2 PETER 5:10: AFTER YOU
HAVE SUFFERED FOR A
WHILE, O   .L
OF KINDNE
WILL GIVE
GLORY, HE
COME AND PICK YOU UP, AND
MAKE YOU STRONGER THAN
EVER.

D1553143

BEYOND DEATH'S DOOR

THE HOPE
FOR REUNION

11/2012

Other books by Gerald Wheeler:
Books of Beginnings
James White: Innovator and Overcomer
*Saints and Sinners: An Insider's Guide to
Bible People and Their Times*

To order, call 1-800-765-6955.

Visit us at **www.reviewandherald.com** for information on other Review and Herald® products.

GERALD WHEELER

BEYOND DEATH'S

DOOR

THE HOPE FOR REUNION

REVIEW AND HERALD® PUBLISHING ASSOCIATION
Since 1861 | www.reviewandherald.com

Published by Review and Herald® Publishing Association, Hagerstown, MD 21741-1119

Review and Herald® titles may be purchased in bulk for educational, business, fund-raising, or sales promotional use. For information, e-mail SpecialMarkets@reviewandherald.com.

The Review and Herald® Publishing Association publishes biblically based materials for spiritual, physical, and mental growth and Christian discipleship.

The author assumes full responsibility for the accuracy of all facts and quotations as cited in this book.

Unless otherwise noted, all Scripture references in this book are from the New Revised Standard Version of the Bible, copyright © 1989 by the Division of Christian Education of the National Council of the Churches of Christ in the U.S.A. Used by permission.

This book was
Edited by Steven S. Winn
Copyedited by James Hoffer
Cover Designed by Trent Truman
Interior Designed by Tina M Ivany
Cover photos by © istockphoto.com/cloudniners/jgroup
Typeset: Bembo 11/13

PRINTED IN U.S.A.

13 12 11 10 09   5 4 3 2 1

Library of Congress Cataloging-in-Publication Data

Wheeler, Gerald.
  Beyond death's door : the hope of reunion / Gerald Wheeler.
    p. cm.
1. Future life—Christianity. 2. Death—Religious aspects—Christianity. 3. Future life. 4. Death. I. Title.
  BT903.W44 2009
  236'.2—dc22
                                        2009014393
ISBN 978-0-8280-2474-7

CONTENTS

CHAPTER 1

SLEEP, MY BELOVED

A faint hum of tires from the nearby freeway filtered through the trees to the cemetery. Exhausted, Jim dropped down on a bench. It took great effort to move. He was not conscious of thought, only of the weight of the questions that pounded through his mind. A foolish question, foolish because there was no answer to it. *What am I going to do? What am I going to do? What am I . . . what am . . . I . . . what . . . ?*

A bird chirped unseen among the blossoms of a nearby mimosa tree, then lapsed into sudden silence. A squirrel, disturbed by Jim's presence, scolded as it dashed across the raw ground of a new grave.

Nan's death had been unexpected. One day she'd mentioned that she was feeling tired and thought she'd lie down for a while. They'd had company recently, and she'd gone all out with cleaning and cooking, and arranging sightseeing for them all. It had been a great two days, but exhausting. No wonder she was tired. But the following day she hadn't gotten up at all. The next events thundered in his mind like a runaway train. Doctors discovered cancer throughout her body. Ten days later Nan was gone.

Jim still couldn't believe it.

Where was the sense in it? Nan's death made no sense. Jim was 10 years older than his wife. He always figured that he'd die first. Where did cancer come from, anyway? How could this enemy creep silently throughout her body until it was too late? A logical man, Jim couldn't understand what had happened. That Nan's death made no sense to him actually deepened his grief.

Then there were the kids. All hell had broken loose since their mom's death. Jack had lost his job—a good job, with great potential—because of the economic downturn. Patti's situation was even worse. Her marriage was over. Shattered. And three little children were drowning in the aftermath.

Jim didn't understand that either. What was wrong with them? In his day people stayed married. So what if you didn't have the same feelings anymore? Didn't young people know that feelings come and go? Where was the commitment? It just made him sick. Patti and Gene. Gene and Patti. Why, they'd been together since they were 18! And the anger! The accusations that had come out in the custody battle made him shake his head.

He'd never say it—never even *think* it. But the truth was that he was glad Nan didn't know about this. Didn't know how scared the grandkids were. Couldn't see their little faces. *Or could she? Was she watching all this from heaven or somewhere?* He buried his face in his hands. *Dear God, how I miss her!*

Then there was Lucy, the baby of the family. Nan had worried herself sick about Lucy. Although their daughter had tried to keep it hidden, she had an alcohol problem, and—no surprise there—it had gotten worse since Nan's death.

An angry row had broken out during the after-funeral dinner. Of course, Lucy had brought her own little bottle and Jack saw it. (Surely she could have gotten through her mother's funeral without it!) *What must Nan think?* But that wasn't the half of it. None of them, himself included, knew how to grieve without taking their pain out on those they loved most.

A soft wind ruffled the grass around Jim's feet. The sun was warm, and could have been comforting if he'd even felt it. But he didn't. His body shivered in the breeze.

Nan's sister had been taking out her grief on him, too. She was angry at death. At least that's what his friend Paul thought. Whatever. Too bad "Death" could-n't hear her hour-long rants. Too bad that Jim also was often the object of them. Poor Nan would feel so bad for him having to deal with Donna, too.

When his heart problem had surfaced, Nan had hovered over him, worrying constantly about his health. "You need a nanny," she'd tease him. "Someone to make sure you behave yourself." He'd always laughed at that, though he tried to follow the doc's orders as best he could. Maybe he sneaked a donut and cup of real coffee now and then, but that was about it. Nan cooked up a storm, making the foods on his restricted diet taste as good as anything he'd ever had before. And now? He didn't have the energy to care what he ate, or when.

Tears filled Jim's eyes. How Nan would grieve to see her beloved family disintegrating so. Lucy! Jack. Patti and Gene and the children. Her own sister. And even him. The question kept hammering at his mind: Did she know it? Was she watching from heaven? Was it all tearing her up as much as it did him?

The squirrel, after watching him for a few minutes, approached Jim slightly, cocking its head to one side as if studying him. Then it chattered to itself again and darted off.

Jim sighed. If it had not been for Paul, it would have been even worse. Paul was not a great talker. He would just squeeze Jim's arm or pat him on the shoulder. Best of all he would sit silently with him as long as Jim wanted. Sometimes his friend would quietly slip him a Bible text. Apparently he sensed Jim's terrible fear that Nan was somehow watching from heaven, or wherever she had gone, as her family shattered and even turned against itself.

Taking a slip of paper out of his pocket, Jim unfolded it, spread it on his knee, and began to read. It had taken him a while to grasp the implications of what his friend had shared with him. But he thought he was at last beginning to understand.

"Consider and answer me, O Lord my God! Give light to my eyes, or I will sleep the sleep of death" (Psalm 13:3).

"Now a certain man was ill, Lazarus of Bethany, the village of Mary and her sister Martha. . . . So the sisters sent a message to Jesus. 'Lord, he whom you love is ill.' . . . [Jesus] told them, 'Our friend Lazarus has fallen asleep, but I am going there to awaken him.' The disciples said to him, 'Lord, if he has fallen asleep, he will be all right.' Jesus, however, had been speaking about his death, but they thought that he was referring merely to sleep. Then Jesus told them plainly, 'Lazarus is dead' (John 11:1-14).

What did it mean that death was like a sleep?

"The living know that they will die, but the dead know nothing; . . . Their love and their hate and their envy have already perished" (Ecclesiastes 9:5, 6).

"Turn O Lord, save my life; deliver me for the sake of your steadfast love. For in death there is no remembrance of you; in Sheol who can give you praise?" (Psalm 6:4, 5).

"You prevail forever against them, and they pass away; . . . Their children come to honor, and they do not know it; they are brought low, and it goes unnoticed" (Job 14:20, 21).

"The dead do not praise the Lord" (Psalm 115:17).

The dead are no longer aware of what happens to the living? Is that what the Bible is trying to tell us? That, in fact, they know nothing?

Jim thought for a long time. Yes, he finally decided, Nan was asleep. She would not see what was happening to her family, would not have to agonize over their grief and the even greater pain for her of not being able to help, to comfort, to make right as she had always done. Then a frightening thought startled Jim. *But is that all there is—an unending sleep? Is death the end of everything we have been to each other?*

He glanced at the paper again, seeking comfort from its words—the words that he had read again and again since Paul had given it to him.

"But we do not want you to be uninformed, brothers and sisters, about those who have died, so that you may not grieve as others do who have no hope. For since we believe that Jesus died and rose again, even so, through Jesus, God will bring with him those who have died. For this we declare to you by the word of the Lord, that we who are alive, who are left until the coming of the Lord, will by no means precede those who have died. For the Lord himself, with a cry of command, with the archangel's call and with the sound of God's trumpet, will descend from heaven and the dead in Christ will rise first. Then we who are alive, who are left, will be caught up in the clouds together with them to meet the Lord in the air; and so we will be with the Lord forever" (1 Thessalonians 4:13-17).

The shadows slowly shifted beneath the trees. Finally, Jim stood and brushed his hand across his eyes.

Sleep, my beloved, until you hear God's wake-up call. I have many questions about this death you are resting in, but I know that I will see you again.

Slipping the sheet of paper back into his pocket, he started for his car. He still wondered about many things. Death was a frightening and mysterious topic. But surely in time he would find enough answers to make some sense of it all.

The unseen bird began to sing again.

CHAPTER 2

THE MYSTERIOUS SLEEP

As his car swept around the sharp curve, Greg John-
son did not see the patch of ice. With a dizzying
sensation, his vehicle slid sideways off the pavement,
then violently straightened, jolted down a steep em-
bankment, and headed toward a massive oak tree. The
front of the car smashed against the trunk of the tree,
abruptly halting its plunge. The last sound Greg heard
was of crumpling metal. His momentum slammed his
chest against the steering wheel. The old car did not
have a functioning air bag. The blow lacerated Greg's
aorta, and blood began to gush into his body cavity.

Minutes later, Greg's blood pressure began to drop.
Attempting to compensate for the reduced blood flow,
his heart began to race. Soon the pressure and amount
of blood reaching Greg's brain became too low, and he
slipped into unconsciousness. The human brain must
constantly have large amounts of oxygen and blood
sugar to sustain it. It has no reserve.

Like a skyscraper cutting the light and heat on each
floor to conserve energy during an emergency, Greg's
brain shut down level after level. First the cerebral cortex failed. The brain stem and medulla held on a little
longer, maintaining respiration, but more and more
ragged. Finally the near-empty heart stopped, fibrillat-
ing for a few minutes before it did so.

Greg did not feel much. For a short time immediately after the impact his brain pumped out endorphins, natural painkillers. Then when he slipped into a coma, it no longer mattered. As the oxygen level plummeted in the brain, its cells filled up with toxins and began to die. A lifetime of memories and skills vanished. Their loss was irreversible. His brain was dead within 15-30 minutes, and other organs soon began to fail and disintegrate. The central nervous system went fast, while the connective tissue of muscle and fibrous structures took longer. The liver cells would continue to function for hours.

Gradually Greg's face took on a gray-white pallor. His eyes, at first glassy and unseeing, within four or five minutes lost their sheen and became dulled as the pupils dilated. Soon the eyeballs would flatten.

He had vanished into that unknown and frightening realm known as death.

Life and death confront us with countless mysteries. They raise questions that humanity has struggled with for thousands of years. Religion, philosophy, and science have offered some answers. In this book we will look at what the Bible says about death and what happens afterward as well as what science is revealing about the nature and workings of the human brain and body.

The Mystery of Death

The abortion controversy of recent years has raised the question of when human life begins. At conception? At birth? Sometime in between?

A perhaps even more difficult issue to define is when life ends and death begins. Physicians used to pronounce someone dead when they could not detect a pulse or heartbeat. Now medical science monitors for brain waves. Life-support systems may keep the heart and circulation going, but if the electrical activity of the brain has stopped, medical science considers the patient brain-dead. But even that criterion may not be reliable. Overdoses of certain addictive drugs can so suppress brain activity that it appears to have ceased altogether. But such individuals can unexpectedly come out of the deep, drug-induced comas.

In recent years physicians have offered new definitions of what constitutes death. One considers people as dead when they enter a persistent vegetative state, a condition that first made news through the controversial case of Karen Ann Quinlan. A later one involving Terri Schiavo created extensive political controversy. Mysteriously, the flow of blood from her heart to her brain was interrupted for at least an hour. The resulting oxygen starvation plunged her into a persistent, vegetative state. After her physical death, x-rays and brain scans revealed that her brain had shriveled to half its size. Her ability to track those around her with her eyes apparently was not conscious action but pure reflex, sometimes called "blindsight," which enables people without any conscious vision to respond to bright lights or moving objects. Although the visual cortex has been destroyed, the optic nerves remain.[1]

Other experts have suggested that we should consider people dead when they have an irreversible loss of memory or can no longer access it, thus losing their personality. The issue is a complex one and may never be resolved.

The Mystery of Life

Perhaps in our attempt to understand the nature of death, we first need to consider something equally complex and mysterious: What is life? At its most fundamental level we might define life as increasing and sustained complexity. A living organism, whether a towering redwood tree, a trumpeting elephant on the savannahs of Africa, or a human being, spends the first part of its existence in a stage of growth. Cells divide and multiply, forming more and more complex tissues, organs, and body systems under the direction of the DNA located in every cell. Such DNA contains unbelievably detailed information that tells a living thing how to become what it must be and then keep itself that way.

A living thing is always an incredibly organized system. Even the individual cells are intricately structured. For most living things that organization steadily increases until the plant or animal reaches its mature form, then levels off. But among human beings the drive for more complexity can continue in the brain until death. The human brain is always organizing and storing memories and other forms of data in the tangle of the synapses connecting the countless cells that make up its matter. Thus, whether it be plant or animal, life is a process of carefully maintained organization and activity.

But as living things age and die, that organization breaks down. DNA no longer replicates itself perfectly. Mistakes creep in. The ends of the strands of DNA making up every cell's chromosomes begin to fray. It is as if the body's instruction manual loses a few pages here and there and the cells no longer have complete backup copies. Interestingly, when scientists clone a sheep or some other living thing, the new organism ages much more rapidly, because its DNA starts at the maturity stage of the creature cloned.

The cells themselves can divide only 50 times, a number known as the Hayflick limit. Then they cease.

As time goes on whole tissues and organs no longer function as efficiently as they once did. Skin structure breaks down and forms wrinkles or sags. Blood vessels clog up, and the immune system weakens. Lungs capture less and less oxygen and hormone levels drop. The brain may deteriorate into dementia. The living thing's level of organization is now declining.

When a plant or animal dies, that breakdown in organization goes into overdrive. Even the microscopic structures of the cells burst and spread their contents throughout the cell. The complex organization that had once been a living thing literally dissolves into a noxious liquid.

As much as science has studied them, both death and life remain mysteries. Where is the exact boundary between life and physical death? The line is difficult to draw. But sooner or later, death always wins.

Is death the end of each human personality? Some think it is, but others cannot accept such a frightening conclusion. Surely life must have more significance than this brief existence. Most cannot imagine that we totally cease at death. Something must continue on.

Some who look at reality solely from a scientific perspective conclude that such a conviction is totally wrong. Jesse Bering argues that our inability to conceive of the mind or personality forever ceasing to exist is nothing more than a quirk of the human brain that evolution has not erased simply because to eliminate it would not endow us with any useful survival value. He claims that recognizing the body of a wild animal or enemy as dead, and thus no longer a threat, helps us function in life, but the acceptance that the mind is no more gives us no useful advantage.[2]

But most readers of this book would instantly reject such a concept. The conviction that the human personality is too precious to accept that it vanishes forever at death is too powerful and compelling to ignore out of hand. Does such a concept have any basis to it?

Let us see first what the Bible has to say.

Death in Scripture

As any reader of Scripture soon realizes, the Bible rarely presents anything in a systematic way. It tells stories, lets psalmists express their feelings, and gives prophetic sermons and letters of pastoral counseling. Reading the latter is sometimes like hearing only one end of a telephone conversation. Often you have to read between the lines to reconstruct the background of the issue under discussion.

Neither the Old Testament nor the New Testament systematically outlines what the human condition in death is like. You have to reconstruct the biblical belief about death from scattered allusions. But while some of the statements can be puzzling, we do notice certain broad positions or concepts. For example, the Bible places definite limitations on how far we can push the imagery it uses to speak about death.

Death in the Old Testament

The ancient Semitic cultures portrayed their ideas of the afterlife through depictions of darkness, silence, and dustiness. The Bible, especially the Old Testament, sometimes uses similar imagery when speaking of death and the dead. The Old Testament often refers to the dead as being in *sheol. Sheol* can indicate either the realm of the dead or the power behind death.[3] Scripture can depict *sheol* as:

A. Dark (Job 10:21; 17:13; 18:18; Psalm 88:12; 143:3; Lamentations 3:6)

B. Dusty and dry (Job 17:16; 21:26; Psalm 7:5)[4]

C. Silent (Psalm 31:17, 18; 94:17; 115:17; Isaiah 47:5)

The Old Testament presents *sheol* as the abode of both the righteous and the wicked (Job 30:23). Only once does it speak of *sheol* in the limited context of dead evildoers (Psalm 9:17). Although the dead may be in *sheol,* they are not beyond God's presence (Psalm 139:8; Proverbs 15:11; Job 26:6; Amos 9:2). The Lord can ransom the dead from it by restoring them to physical life (Psalm 16:10; 30:3; 49:15; 86:13; Job 33:18, 28-30). The Bible writers depicted *sheol* deep within the earth (Psalm 88:6; Ezekiel 26:20; 31:15; Amos 9:2). It could be personified as a hungry beast (Proverbs 27:20; Isaiah 5:14; Habakkuk 2:5) with an open mouth and insatiable appetite, reminding one of the descriptions of the Canaanite god of death, Mot.[5]

As for the dead themselves, the very most we can infer from the Old Testament is their portrayal as little more than shadows. But as we shall see later, the fundamental limitations that the Old Testament imposes on them makes even that shadowiness impossible.

Notice that even these images appear as brief allusions in poetic passages, cautioning us not to push their literality too far. The same principle applies to longer passages.

In Isaiah 14:9-20 and Ezekiel 32, for example, the writers have the dead making comments about the newly arrived deceased. The biblical authors are probably using the Semitic tradition of the afterlife to ridicule the attitudes of the surrounding cultures. Neither chapter has as its goal a formal description of the abode of the dead. The intent seems to be the symbolization of the powerlessness of God's enemies. The depictions are literary devices that both Israelites and non-Israelites would understand, not systematic expositions of doctrine. And even at that, the afterlife they describe is quite different from the popular understanding of a fiery hell projected into certain passages of the New Testament or the bliss of heaven imagined by so many today..

The Old Testament writers may have employed familiar and widespread imagery from surrounding cultures that did believe in a conscious afterlife. But they did so with their own particular twist—a perspective that helps us understand both what they meant and what they did not intend to say. Some years ago, Alexander Heidel compared what the Old Testament said about the dead with Mesopotamian concepts of an afterlife.[6] He found a number of fundamental differences that help us interpret biblical statements about death. (Egyptian religion shared some characteristics with that of Mesopotamia.) The contrasts between biblical and pagan religion include:

1. Mesopotamian religion asserted that the gods created death as a natural part of the order of things for human beings. The Old Testament taught that God created human beings with the intent of having them live forever. Death was not part of God's plan for them. (We will look at the biblical explanation for the origin of death later.)

2. Mesopotamian religion had special gods ruling the world of the dead. The God of Israel governed both the living and the dead.

3. The Mesopotamians considered both the living and the dead as dependent upon each other. The living had to feed the dead, and the dead in turn could either help or harm the living because they knew what was happening in the world above. The Old Testament clearly emphasized that the dead know nothing about what happens to the living.[7] (We will discuss this more a bit later.)

4. Mesopotamian religion knows nothing about the concept of resurrection of the body. While a god (such as Baal) might escape the underworld, no human being ever did. The books of Daniel and Isaiah do, however, present the first major hints of the doctrine of resurrection. (The topic of resurrection will be examined later.)

"These differences," Heidel concludes, "set the eschatology of the Mesopotamians and that of the Hebrews as far apart as the east is from the west."[8]

In addition to these differences, the Old Testament places stringent limitations on the dead. Such boundaries, for all practical purposes, make it impossible for us to interpret the imagery that the Old Testament writers use as anything other than literary vehicles to present the author's point or teaching. They do not depict reality, except in the most general sense. Whatever the fate of the dead may be, according to Scripture it cannot violate the following criteria:

1. The dead remember nothing of their human life (Psalm 6:5; 88:12).
2. The dead have no thoughts (Ecclesiastes 9:10; Psalm 146:4).
3. The dead do not speak (Psalm 31:17; 94:17) or praise God (Psalm 6:5; 30:9).
4. The dead know nothing of what happens in the world of the living (Job 14:21; Ecclesiastes 9:10).[9]
5. The dead can no longer work (Ecclesiastes 9:10).
6. The dead can no longer participate in human life or influence what takes place among the living (Ecclesiastes 9:6).
7. The dead of both human beings and of animals perish in the same way (Ecclesiastes 3:19-21).[10]

Joel B. Green summarizes it succinctly. "For Israel's Scriptures, death is never a question merely of biological cessation. Though the books of the OT provide some variation in their perspectives on death, we may nonetheless speak of common threads. These would include at least three affirmations—first, human existence is marked by finitude; second, death is absolute; and third, death is regarded as the sphere within which fellowship with Yahweh is lost."[11]

If the dead do not think, speak, remember, or know anything, they cannot have any form of consciousness that we could understand. How, then, can we possibly say that they any longer have any meaningful form of existence?

Note that many of the texts cited come from the book of Ecclesiastes, a writing rather pessimistic in its outlook. Some try to downplay the book's statements about the nature of death by protesting that the passages are just the mutterings of a perhaps depressed individual. Ecclesiastes is gloomy at times as its author struggles with deep and complex questions. But if the dead are not really unconscious and unaware of life on earth (Ecclesiastes 9:5, 6), if the righteous and the wicked do not share the same fate at death (Ecclesiastes 6:6; 9:2), and if human beings and animals do not have the same condition at death (Ecclesiastes 3:19-21), the Preacher's (as he calls himself) comparisons are meaningless and his arguments collapse. However, the author *is* presenting fundamental truth and reality. Otherwise, why does the Bible include the book at all?

Others might argue that the literality of the psalms must not be pushed too far. While that is true, again, the psalmist's message would be meaningless if there were no truth at all to his comparisons and figures of speech. We must take seriously these scriptural limitations on the dead.

Unlike the elaborate portrayals of the underworld found in Egyptian tomb paintings and scrolls and in Mesopotamian documents, the Bible has almost nothing to say about *sheol*.[12] This fact should caution us against using its few allusions to the dead to construct a detailed doctrine of an afterlife. The Bible writers seem more interested in what the dead are *not* than in whatever they might be. Even more important, they focus on what the living must do to come into relationship with God before they die.

Many scholars, even though they may personally believe in a conscious afterlife, are careful to make clear that the Old Testament does not teach the popular Christian understanding of where people go after they die. The author remembers the noted Catholic priest and scholar Roland Murphy prefacing a presentation on the wisdom literature (Proverbs, Job, and similar books) of the Bible. Murphy emphasized that while one might hold the traditional Christian views of the afterlife, one must also recognize that the Old Testament simply did not teach them.

Others are uncomfortable with the Old Testament's restricted depiction of the dead. As an example, Robert A. Morey protested the "undue dependence upon Old Testament texts" of those who reject a conscious state of the dead.[13] He argued that progressive revelation means that we must interpret Old Testament passages in light of the greater New Testament understanding. But the Old Testament was the Scripture of Christ and the early Christian church, and as we shall see, the New Testament was more in harmony with the Old Testament in its outlook on death than most have recognized.

The Origin of Death

The Old Testament describes the nature or condition of death only briefly, and it just as succinctly mentions its origin. Rather than going into great detail, it restricts itself to telling a simple but profound story and then lets the reader ponder its implications.

After God created the first humans He gave them a special place to live, the Garden of Eden. Everything in it belonged to them—except for just one thing. "Of the tree of the knowledge of good and evil you shall not eat, for in the day that you eat of it you shall die" (Genesis 2:17). God had allowed them the use of every part of a good creation and set off-limits only one tree, hardly a heavy burden.

Scripture does not go into extensive theological or scientific explanations of what happened at the tree of good and evil. Genesis left much for later revelation to unfold, and even more remains unknown until we meet God face to face.

Genesis 3:1 states tersely that "the serpent was more crafty than any other wild animal that the Lord God had made." The biblical author does not explain how a being that was part of a physical creation God joyfully called "good" (Genesis 1:31) could turn against its Creator. Nor does it tell us how and why it led the human couple, who were supposed to have dominion over it, into disobedience. The New Testament does offer clues to the working of a greater serpent, but Genesis is more interested in how the couple willingly rushed into rebellion against the Creator.

The woman—she is not yet named—encounters the serpent one day. "Did God say," it asks her, "You shall not eat from any tree in the garden?" (verse 1). Of course, the Creator had never said any such thing. The serpent uses a big lie to set the woman up. It makes a distortion so great in one direction that the woman un-wittingly swings to the other extreme in her effort to correct it.

"We may eat of the fruit of the trees in the gar-den," she replies, "but God said, 'You shall not eat of the fruit of the tree that is in the middle of the garden, nor shall you touch it, or you shall die'" (verses 2, 3). The woman added to God's command, making it stricter than it was.

The serpent's misquoting of God's command has planted in the human being's mind the possibility of an alternative to doing what their Creator asked them to do. If the couple had obeyed the divine command, they would have known what it was to trust Him. Instead, by listening to the serpent and then doing what it suggested, they came to know only distrust.

At first glance what the serpent says next seems to change the topic. But it is really the goal toward which the being had been progressing all along. The creature tells her, "You will not die;[14] for God knows that when you eat of it your eyes will be opened, and you will be like God, knowing good and evil" (verses 4, 5).[15]

The human couple eat the forbidden fruit, especially since "the tree was to be desired to make one wise" (verse 6). The man and woman craved wisdom—but they learned only shame and fear (verses 7, 8). Our first parents longed to be gods, but only had their god-likeness—the image of God they already possessed (Genesis 2:27)—tragically tarnished. They had used their freedom—part of that image—and transformed it into disobedience and slavery to fear and death. They had sinned. Sin leads to disorder and chaos in every aspect of life. And death is the ultimate disorder.

Death in the New Testament

The Old Testament, while it acknowledged in Genesis 2 and 3 that death was not part of God's original plan, still treated it as a normal conclusion to life, though we have seen some exceptions such as Ecclesiastes 9:3.[16] People lived a good life, honored God, and were buried with their ancestors. The Hebrew Scriptures only rarely alluded to the possibility of resurrection. Children carried on the family name since no one came back from the grave.

The New Testament, however, regards death with greater horror. The disciples cry out in fear of death during the storm on the Sea of Galilee (Matthew 8:23-27; Mark 4:35-41; Luke 8:22-25). Matthew 4:16 and Luke 1:79 employ the phrase "shadow of death" in a negative sense. Jesus raises the dead and cries at Lazarus's death. Christ approaches His own death with anguish. (Matthew 26:36-44; 27:46; Mark 14:32-39; 15:34; Luke 22:39-44). New Testament writers more fully elaborate the idea that God did not create humanity to die. Death stalks us because of human sin and disobedience. "The wages of sin is death" (Romans 6:23). Adam brought it upon the human race (Romans 5:16, 18; 1 Corinthians 15:21), and it ultimately claims all (Hebrews 9:27). The New Testament also links it with judgment, especially that of the wicked (Romans 2:1-11; Revelation 20:6; 21:8).

But while death was not meant to be, Christ has dealt with it. He reversed the curse that Adam inflicted on humanity (Romans 5:10) and brought us life instead of death (verse 18). His crucifixion destroyed "the one who has the power of death, that is, the devil" (Hebrews 2:14). The New Testament closely associates Satan and death. And whereas the Old Testament connected sin with death (Ezekiel 18:4, 20), the New Testament details the relationship (Romans 3:23; 5:12-21). But even beyond that, it sees Christ as the solution to both problems. His death not only gave us forgiveness of our sins but also "abolished death and brought life and immortality to light through the gospel" (2 Timothy 1:10). Unlike that of fallen human beings, His death could not hold Him in the grave (Acts 2:24). Christ's death and resurrection entitled Him to "be Lord of both the dead and the living" (Romans 14:9). As our Savior and because He passed through death, He has "the keys of Death and of Hades" (Revelation 1:18).

Perhaps most important of all, the New Testament views death within the context of Jesus' resurrection. The Greek adjective for "dead" is *nekros*. Seventy-five times *nekros* is the object of *egeiro* ("to awaken") or *anastasis* ("to rise"). The New Testament calls Christ the firstborn of the dead in the sense that He was the most important to rise from the grave (Colossians 1:18; Revelation 1:5). Even if death does happen, it does not separate us from Christ (Romans 8:38, 39). Thus Paul can use such imagery when referring to death as being "at home with the Lord" (2 Corinthians 5:8) as "gain" (Philippians 1:21), and "to depart and be with Christ" (verse 23). In each case he is saying that we need not worry about death since neither it nor anything in life can come between us and God. It is his way of describing his confidence in Christ and His plan of salvation, not any hypothetical intermediary stage between death and the resurrection. "Simply put, Paul pictures the Christian's death as nonfinal and nonthreatening."[17] This is imagery that must not be forced, especially not into a doctrine that contradicts the rest of biblical teaching on the nature of death and the dead. Without Christ, death is threatening and final.

What about a passage such as 1 Peter 3:19, in which Christ "made proclamation to the spirits now in prison"? Tradition has long held that Christ went to hell during His burial and preached to the dead there. Paul J. Achtemeier, however, presents a growing scholarly consensus that Christ's proclamation in this passage took place not between His death and resurrection, but after the Resurrection. The "spirits" were not the souls of the dead, but evil powers, and Christ did not preach the gospel to them, but judged them in light of the cross.[18] Also, Achtemeier regards the dead in 1 Peter 4:6 as Christians who had accepted the gospel before their death, and the cross provides assurance that they will rise at the resurrection and live with God.[19]

The New Testament also uses death as a symbol of sin and its effects. One can be "dead in sin" (Ephesians 2:1; Colossians 2:13; Revelation 3:1) or a prisoner of the power of sin (Romans 7:24). Conversion to Christ, the release from the bondage of sin, becomes a rebirth (Romans 6:5-11; Galatians 2:20).

But though we all face the prospect of death until Christ's return, those who are "in Christ" have the promise of God's gift of immortality. It is an indomitable hope (Romans 8:31-38; 1 Corinthians 15:58; 1 Thessalonians 4:18), because we know that we will be "made alive" (1 Corinthians 15:22). Thus the focus shifts from death itself to resurrection, to the power of Christ to overcome death, and to the believer's need to accept Christ.

The Imagery of Death as Sleep

In the previous chapter we began to see that the

31

Bible frequently uses the imagery of sleep as a way of referring to death. Scripture says of the various kings of Israel and Judah that after death they slept with their ancestors (for example: 1 Kings 2:10; 11:43; 14:20, 31; 15:8; 2 Chronicles 21:1). Job (Job 7:21; 14:10-12), David the psalmist (Psalm 13:3), Jeremiah (Jeremiah 51:39, 57), and Daniel (Daniel 12:2) called death a sleep.

The New Testament continues the imagery. Jesus told the mourners that Jairus's dead daughter was sleeping (Matthew 9:24; Mark 5:39), as He did of His beloved friend Lazarus (John 11:11-14). At Christ's death, some tombs opened during an earthquake "and many bodies of the saints who had fallen asleep were raised. After his resurrection they came out of the tombs and entered the holy city and appeared to many" (Matthew 27:52, 53). In the Greek, Luke describes the stoning death of Stephen as a falling asleep (Acts 7:60). Paul and Peter employed the same tradition in 1 Corinthians 15:6, 51, 52; 1 Thessalonians 4:13-17; and 2 Peter 3:4. It is for this reason that a burial place is called a cemetery, which originally meant a sleeping place.

To the ancients sleep was a mystery. What happened to the consciousness during it? Where did the soul go during dreaming? Today we know that sleep is only a reduced state of consciousness, that the brain is still active during it. Sleeping people dream. Thus it could be tempting to some moderns to regard the "sleep" of death as an intermediate state between the present life and the final life. Do the dead experience some equivalent of dreaming? Some commentators have suggested so. But that is projecting modern understandings of sleep into the ancient imagery. We must not push the imagery beyond what the biblical writers intended. It is better to restrict the idea of death to the way the ancients would have viewed it—a state of non-being, a condition in which we are unable to act or do. In sleep we are unconscious of the world around us. Death, Scripture tells us, is something like that. But what is the soul and what happens to it? We will answer that question in the next chapter.

---

[1] www.washingtonpost.com/wp-dyn/content/article/2005/06/15/AR2005061500512.html. Cf. Bob Stein, "Even a Blind Man Can See: Input From Eyes May Get Rerouted in Brain," Washington *Post*, Dec. 23, 2008.

[2] Jesse Bering, "The End?" *Scientific Mind* (October/November 2008), pp. 34-41.

[3] D. N. Freedman, ed., *Anchor Bible Dictionary* (New York: Doubleday, 1992), vol. 2, p. 101.

[4] Some passages do speak of water imagery, as in Jonah 2:3-6; Psalms 42:7; 69:2, 3, 15, 16; and 88:7, 8. The New Testament introduces the imagery of fire. However, the New Testament does retain the image of dryness and dustiness in Christ's parable of the return of the unclean spirit (Luke 11:24). These various figures of speech make a most puzzling range of images, suggesting that death is ultimately like none of them.

[5] Ancient Ugaritic texts describe Mot as the archenemy of Baal, leader of the gods. At one point Mot traps Baal in the underworld, and Baal has to be rescued. The story became the mythic explanation of the rainy and dry seasons of Palestine. Baal is imprisoned in the underworld during the dry season or times of drought, but rain and fertility return when he is released. Habakkuk 2:5 and Job 18:13, 14, particularly use imagery that reminds us of the ravenous Mot (see *Anchor Bible Dictionary,* vol. 4, pp. 922-924).

[6] Alexander Heidel, *The Gilgamesh Epic and Old Testament Parallels* (Chicago: University of Chicago Press, 1963), pp. 170-223.

[7] *Ibid.,* pp. 222, 223.

[8] *Ibid.,* p. 223.

[9] As we noted in the first chapter, this means that the dead are spared the agony of seeing what happens to their loved ones after the deceased have passed off the scene.

[10] R. E. Murphy, *Ecclesiastes, Word Biblical Commentary* (Dallas: Word Books, 1992), vol. 23A, p. 37.

[11] Joel B. Green, Body, *Soul, and Human Life: The Nature of Humanity in the Bible* (Grand Rapids: Baker Academic, 2008), p. 147.

[12] *Anchor Bible Dictionary,* vol. 2, p. 102.

[13] Robert A. Morey, *Death and the Afterlife* (Minneapolis: Bethany House Publishers, 1984), pp. 23, 215.

[14] The serpent's claim is only partially correct. They do not immediately die. But it is not because of the serpent's doing, only God's.

[15] Again the serpent is partially correct (cf. Genesis 3:22) as the creature mixes truth and falsehood.

[16] Murphy, pp. lxvii, pp. 38, 91.

[17] Butler, ed., *Holman Bible Dictionary,* p. 348.

[18] Paul J. Achtemeier, *I Peter: A Commentary on First Peter* (Minneapolis: Fortress, 1996), pp. 252-262.

[19] *Ibid.,* pp. 290, 291.

CHAPTER 3

WHAT IS A SOUL?

As Americans began building the first railroads across the rugged landscapes of New England, they found it to be hard and dangerous work. Early nineteenth-century construction crews had only pickaxes, shovels, and other primitive tools. For much of the century they used nothing more powerful than black gunpowder to blast their way through rock. The men pulverized the hillsides and bore tunnels and cuts through the ridges by first drilling a hole into the rock, then tamping the gunpowder into it with a metal rod. Unfortunately, the gunpowder sometimes ignited prematurely as the laborer rammed it in, or he might forget to remove the rod when he finished. In either case, the explosive would hurl the rod into the air like a harpoon.

In 1848 25-year-old Phineas P. Gage worked as a construction foreman on the Rutland & Burlington Railroad in Vermont. A dependable and shrewd businessperson, he was well liked by his men and supervisors. Then an accident on September 13 changed everything. An explosion thrusted a 13-pound tamping rod measuring three feet seven inches by one and a quarter inches into his cheek under his left eye and up through his skull just above the hairline.[1] But the missile did not kill him, even though he lost some brain tissue. To the amazement of everyone, Gage managed to sit up, the rod still impaled in his head. As the shock wore off from the blow, he began to speak coherently. A doctor removed the rod, and Gage recovered.

At first Phineas seemed normal. But then people started to notice some differences about him. Gage was no longer the likeable person he had been before the accident. That personality had vanished. Now Phineas was fickle, foul-mouthed, and irresponsible to the point that he could no longer hold a job. He became a drifter. For a time he may have been one of P.T. Barnum's sideshow exhibits. Sadly, his friends wondered at the man who had turned into a restless, obnoxious, and impulsive caricature of his former self. "Gage was no longer Gage," they commented among themselves.[2] And it was true. Because his brain was no longer the same, neither was he.

The personality of Phineas Gage had dramatically altered because the tamping rod had sliced through the frontal cortex of his brain. The destruction of the brain tissue had forever erased part of his personality. The now missing areas of his brain normally guide decision-making and restrain impulsiveness. (The frontal regions of the brain are among the last to mature, and do not fully develop until adulthood. That is why teenagers indulge in such risky behavior.) With that control center of his brain gone, other less desirable traits took over and dominated Gage's personality. His injury also severely affected his ability to maintain social relationships. He was now more comfortable working with horses than with human beings, and for many years he drove a Conestoga stagecoach in the country of Chile. Although his life was tragic, his traumatic accident provided some of the first clues to the intricate relationship between mind and body and that injury to the brain can alter human personality.

Medical and psychological researchers have learned much since then about how the brain works. Injuries to the brain such as Gage's, as well as strokes, have taught science what many of its parts do. The horrendous wounds caused by the fighting between the Germans and Russians allowed the Russian physicians treating the casualties to discover even more about the functioning of each area of the brain. In addition, neuroscientists have conducted endless experiments on normal brains and acquired even greater understanding of their functioning. Such discoveries have answered many questions about the nature of the human mind.

Human beings have not always considered the brain as vital as we do today. The ancient Egyptians did not regard it as of much significance. They believed that the dead would not continue to exist in the afterlife if their physical bodies were not carefully preserved in the tomb. But when Egyptians mummified the dead, they extracted the tissue of the brain and threw it away. The Greeks saw a little more use for the brain. Aristotle believed that it served as a radiator for the body, cooling the blood.

Today, science recognizes the central role of the brain in making us alive, conscious, and human. Let us look at some of the amazing discoveries that science has made about that three-pound mass of grayish matter that fills our skulls.

The Amazing Brain

The brain is the most incredibly complex part of the entire human body. As it develops, its cells send out finger-like extensions called dendrites to each other to form an increasingly organized network. Each neuron may link up with as many as 15,000 others, creating trillions of possible connections.

Some areas of the brain regulate various bodily processes, including breathing, digestion, and the production and release of hormones. Other regions store the memories. UCLA neuroscientists and a team of researchers measured the electrical activity in areas of the brains of 13 volunteers as each one watched video clips of television programs. Then the scientists asked the study participants to describe whichever video segment popped into their mind. The monitoring of their brain activity revealed that the same neurons fired that had done so when they had watched the specific video they now recollected. Because the neurons start firing a few seconds before a person becomes aware of a memory, the researchers knew which video clip the participant would talk about even before they did. The study confirms that the brain stores memories in specific neurons, and when they reactivate, we remember the memory stored in them.[3] Human beings house their past history—their lives—in the microscopic web of interlinked brain cells.

And still other parts of the brain's amazing network of cells process the thoughts and emotions that make up the human personality. The brain handles emotions in specific areas of the brain. For example, two structures in the frontal cortex—the putamen and insula—form a "hate circuit" that is active when we experience this particular emotion. Interestingly, the putamen and the insula also are involved when a person feels romantic love,[4] indicating that the two emotions are closely linked.

When you Google something on the Internet, the company's computers break your search into bits and pieces and send each fragment to dedicated computers that handle that specific area, searching for links to the requested data. Other computers evaluate the various links through highly involved algorithms and select the ones that seem most relevant. All the computers work simultaneously.

Working in a similar manner, but at an even more complex level, the human brain breaks down data into tiny segments stored in many places, then retrieves them through the coordination of several areas that we might compare to subprocessing units in a computer.

The body's DNA tells the developing embryo to form the connections that make up all these regions. They are "hardwired" in the brain. But if during the first few months of life the new circuits do not receive regular stimulation, many of them will atrophy and die. The brain "assumes" that they are not needed. Thus, a baby born with cataracts and left untreated for as little as six months will be forever blind. The visual region of the infant's brain will wither away from lack of use. And the brain will lose the ability to process vision. That is why constant visual and other sensory stimulation is vital for infants.

The human brain, researchers have found, thus stores memories in the web of neurons. If anything affects the neurons, such as disease or physical trauma, the memories can either be blocked so that the mind cannot receive them, or they may be destroyed forever.

Krickitt and Kim Carpenter had been married for 10 weeks when an automobile accident caused severe bleeding in Krickitt's brain. She survived, but lost all her memories for 18 months before the accident and for four months afterward. Unfortunately, she had met her husband during those missing initial 18 months.

Kim was now a complete stranger to her. They had to court each other all over again. In addition, she had to relearn many things from eating to taking a shower. The accident had also damaged areas of her brain that contained her personality. Her bubbly nature vanished. In time a new personality emerged, one with significant differences. The two of them were lucky. The divorce rate of couples in which one of them has sustained a brain trauma is between 80 and 90 percent. The changes in personality are often more than the other spouse can handle.[5]

Brain damage can also prevent the formation of new memories. Oliver Sacks recorded the case of a man with a slow-growing tumor that destroyed the hippocampus area and its adjacent cortex. The patient lost the ability to record new memories. The tumor also wiped out regions with already existing memories, so that he could remember nothing beyond the 1960s.[6] In an earlier case, Sacks studied how alcoholism had wiped out the memories in a sailor's brain extending back to his youth. Even though he was a gray-haired man, eventually he knew nothing beyond 1945, when he had been 19 or 20. A few minutes after something happened to him, he would permanently forget it.[7]

The fact that we store memories in the biochemical structure of the brain may someday allow us to erase traumatic ones. Research on the brains of mice suggests that manipulation of an enzyme known as CaMKII seems to remove unwanted memories. Forcing an overproduction of the enzyme, the researchers caused the lab animal to recall an unpleasant experience then eliminated it from its memory without affecting other memories.[8] Only time will tell whether human beings will be able to excise unwanted memories, but such research again reminds us of the biochemical nature of those very memories.

We see another example of how personality resides in the brain in the case of a businessperson named Elliot. Elliot had surgery to remove a brain tumor from the prefrontal cortex, an area essential to decision-making. Though his intelligence remained unaffected, he lost the ability to experience emotion. Without emotion, strange as it may seem, the man could no longer behave *rationally,* and his business career disintegrated.

Antonio Damasio, who treated Elliot, points out that emotion is a key part of learning and making decisions. When an investment fails, emotion causes the person to feel bad and thus act with greater care the next time. But no matter how wrong his decisions, Elliot could not learn from the experiences because he had no emotional reaction. "We can't decide whom we're going to marry, what savings strategy to adopt, where to live, on the basis of reason alone," Damasio explains.[9]

Subtly different levels of certain chemicals in various parts of the brain can drastically shape how we act. Shortage of serotonin, a chemical that helps us decide to avoid a behavior that has previously led to punishment, can result in a person getting into all kinds of trouble. Low levels of serotonin in the frontal lobes and limbic system seem to permit more impulsive behavior. Above-normal levels of norepinephrine make people respond irrationally to every perceived slight or make them unable to resist the desire to buy everything they see.[10] Dopamine highs may be a part of falling in love. Those who have high concentrations in the brain are more likely to take great risks, such as driving too fast, competing in extreme sports, gambling, overspending, or drinking too much.[11]

The mind is not independent of the brain. Drugs, disease, the health of the rest of the body—all influence the personality. And it can work in reverse. The consciousness can even affect the physical nature of the brain, as we see in discoveries of how obsessive-compulsive disorder (OCD) works.

People with OCD find themselves driven to repeat certain behaviors again and again. Millions of Americans are victims of such urges as checking to make sure their appliances are turned off, or washing their hands constantly. Such actions result from a malfunction in the area of the brain known as the caudate nucleus. The region serves as a kind of gearshift for processing thought. When it fails to shift, the part of the brain called the orbital cortex gets locked up. The orbital cortex tells the rest of the brain that something needs to be done. According to psychiatrist Jeffrey Schwartz, the feeling that something needs to be, for example, checked or washed will then not go away.

Medical science has used Prozac or a similar drug

to treat OCD. Some patients do not respond to medication, however, and for those who do, the symptoms return as soon as they stop taking the drug. But research indicates that behavior modification can remodel the brain and stop or lessen OCD. It had obsessive-compulsive victims tell themselves that they were experiencing an OCD behavior resulting from a chemical imbalance in the brain. Then they concentrated for at least 15 minutes on some other activity, such as gardening, playing a musical instrument, or knitting.

"By engaging another part of the brain, the caudate gets unstuck and shifts out of the pattern that insists" on the particular OCD behavior.[12] Not all OCD patients were able to modify their behavior, but for those who did, positron emission tomography (PET) scans of their brains revealed definite biochemical changes after such behavior modification.[13] The brain was rewiring its biological circuits.

Brain and body are intricately interconnected. The brain not only controls the functions of the rest of the body, but that body in turn influences the brain in a number of ways. Emotions arising in the mind affect physiological activities in the tissues and organs throughout the body, while substances known as neuropeptides act as messengers between the immune system and the mind, influencing such things as moods and resistance to disease. Thus emotions such as joy and contentment can help the body fight off disease while grief and guilt make it more vulnerable to it. On the other hand, the neuropeptides and other substances alter the moods and behavior of the mind that reside in the brain.[14] Mind and body are in constant communication with each other, and each new finding of science reveals that they are indivisible. Studies of the placebo effect have presented an interesting example. The drug morphine depresses respiration. Researchers gave patients taking morphinelike drugs for pain a placebo. The patients' brains, now used to the respiratory depression caused by the real drug, now triggered the same physiological reaction. The same kind of thing happens when placebos are substituted for other drugs.

All that we are as human beings is shaped by what is contained in those fragile tissues and biochemicals of the brain. We are the product of the matter between our ears. And anything that affects that brain directly impacts who we are. The brain is the storage system preserving our personalities and the memories that help make up those personalities. Lose that miraculous storage and processing system, and we would no longer be us. That is what happened to Phineas Gage.

As long as it lives, the brain maintains the intricate data that make each one of us unique. It is constantly modifying itself as we grow not only physically but intellectually and emotionally. The brain not only preserves information, memories, and traits that constitute who we are, but also generates new data as we think and respond to the world around us. And it is self-aware as it does so.

Shape-shifters and Disappearing Loved Ones

Science fiction likes to explore all kinds of ideas about mind and consciousness. The popular *Star Trek* series employed such concepts as mind transfer and characters who were "shape-shifters." Athena Andreadis, a fan of the programs and an assistant professor of neurology at Harvard Medical School, wrote a book to examine these and other ideas in the series. Discussing the mind-body relationship as it concerned the possibility of actual mind transfer or shape-shifting, she concluded that neither was possible.[15] Mind, she emphasized, is tied to neural structure. A shape-shifter would lose its neural structure, and the mind, as far as science can tell, cannot exist independently of some kind of brain. She rejected the idea that consciousness can survive apart from the physical structure of the brain. Although she was a fan of the shows, she concluded that many of the concepts in them were more New Age than scientific. And here is where all that we have been discussing touches upon our question of What is a soul?

The inseparable connections we have repeatedly seen between mind and body have fundamental implications for such popular theories as a self-existing soul or reincarnation. For example, what happens as loved ones disappear into the ravages of Alzheimer's disease and other forms of dementia? Are their souls trapped inside them, watching in horror as their outward personality ceases to exist?

As the brain's neural structures break down, the personality contained in them slowly ceases to be. We could compare it to a pencil portrait of a person. As we erase random bits of the drawing here and there, we continue to recognize the individual in the portrait. But eventually, as we remove more and more of the lines of the drawing, it becomes increasingly difficult to "see" the face. Finally, when we eradicate too many of the details, the face vanishes altogether.

The personality of an individual ravaged by brain disease does not become confined somewhere, helplessly watching the now bizarre and frustrating antics of the body. The personhood simply ceases to exist at all. We are our brains, and when they are gone, so are we.

That Three-pound Universe

From the moment that the first few neural cells divide in the developing embryo until the onset of death the brain has been constantly weaving itself into ever-more intricate patterns. It is in that fantastic neural maze that we experience our lives. Our mind-body unity can never be severed apart from death.

Michael Craig Miller, editor-in-chief of the *Harvard Mental Health Letter,* observes that the brain consisting of 100 billion nerve cells that individually do not have the ability to reason or feel emotion, yet when working together can produce what we know as consciousness. "For about 400 years, following the ideas of French philosopher René Descartes, those who thought about its nature considered the mind related to the body, but separate from it. In this model—often called 'dualism' or the mind-body problem—the mind was 'immaterial,' not anchored in anything physical. Today neuroscientists are finding abundant evidence . . . that separating mind from brain makes no sense. Nobel Prize-winning psychiatrist-neuroscientist Eric Kandel stated it directly in a watershed paper published in 1998: 'All mental processes, even the most complex psychological processes, derive from operations of the brain.'"[16]

Miller goes on to add that "your heart, lungs, kidneys, and digestive tract keep you alive. But your brain is where you live. The brain is responsible for most of what you care about—language, creativity, imagination, empathy, and morality. And it is the repository of all that you feel."[17]

Of Many Minds

Unlike the desktop computers that can handle only one task at a time, the brain enables us to breathe, walk, chew gum, and talk all at the same time. Our brains are collections of subprocessing units that simultaneously control our body functions and do our thinking. Some of those parts of the brain are so complex that they function as discrete centers of conscious or unconscious mental activity.

A type of research known as split-brain studies has revealed that the right and left hemispheres have separate consciousnesses. Because they work so well together and constantly share information with each other, we are never aware of this fact except for such situations as when we discover that we have been humming to ourselves for some time but were not aware of it. Research on a number of individuals who had the nerves between the hemispheres surgically severed to stop an extreme form of epilepsy revealed the existence of the two centers of consciousness.[18]

Once the author was trying to think of someone's name but kept drawing a blank. Then he realized that he had been repeating the name aloud to himself for a second or two. The right and left hemispheres duplicate most mental processes, but the speech center is an exception. It exists in only one side of the brain. Each person has a dominant hemisphere in which they do much of their conscious thinking. As the author sought to remember the name, he was using the hemisphere without the speech center to search for the elusive name. But the side of the brain with the capacity for speech found the name and led him to say it out loud.

The brain also works on an unconscious level. Scientists suggest that 90 percent of the brain's thinking and reasoning capacity may operate in the unconsciousness. Some experts suggest that if you are trying to solve some difficult problem or remember some forgotten fact and aren't getting anywhere, stop consciously focusing on it. Instead, think of something else for a while and let the unconsciousness tackle it with that greater part of the brain's capacity. Perhaps you have had the experience of lying in bed and all kinds of ideas or solutions to problems suddenly begin rushing through your mind. You have relaxed your consciousness enough for the unconscious areas of your brain—which have been busy retrieving facts, solving problems, composing a writing assignment, or whatever—to finally get the attention of your conscious awareness.

If you ever wonder if the subconscious exists, think about the last time you drove somewhere and afterward remembered nothing about the trip. One part of your brain took care of the steering and braking while another part mused on its own thoughts.

What has all this discussion about the wonders of the brain, you may be wondering, have to do with the question, What is the soul?

It can no longer be denied that thinking and consciousness—the awareness and personality that make us what we are—are the product of the biochemical activity of our neural structures. This reality is especially demonstrated by the fact that disease, physical injury, or anything else that damages or alters that complex structure will lessen that consciousness, as we sadly have seen happen to those who underwent the operation known as the lobotomy.[19] Enough damage, and the person then simply ceases to exist.

Implications of an Immortal Soul

But popular opinion believes in an immortal soul independent of the body. It is the soul, many assume, that provides intelligence and consciousness. In the examples I have given above, which of the various consciousnesses is the soul? The right or left hemisphere? Or both? And what about the subconscious? Does each hemisphere of the brain have its own as split-brain studies might suggest? Furthermore, research has shown that the brain has processes of which we are not consciously aware that can sometimes take control of our behavior—that there is much more of us than we realize.[20] These hidden abilities of the mind can make decisions just like the consciousness. Would they also be part of that soul?

The body may die, most assume, but the spiritual soul, freed of the constraints of physical matter, then goes to its eternal reward. Such an idea may seem comforting, but what does a body animated by such a hypothetical soul really mean?

Steven Pinker, a leader in brain research, observed some years ago that "the traditional explanation of intelligence is that human flesh is suffused with a nonmaterial entity, the soul, usually envisioned as some kind of ghost or spirit. But the theory faces an insur-mountable problem: How does the spook interact with solid matter? How does an ethereal nothing respond to flashes, pokes, and beeps and get arms and legs to move? Another problem is the overwhelming evidence that the mind is the activity of the brain. The supposedly immortal soul, we now know, can be bisected with a knife, altered by chemicals, started or stopped by elec-tricity, and extinguished by a sharp blow or insufficient oxygen. Under the microscope the brain has a breath-taking complexity of physical structures fully commen-surate with the richness of mind."[21]

Others might suggest that the physical body creates a soul as it grows and develops, impressing upon its in-visible substance the individual's personality. The im-material soul is an indestructible record of the physical (neural) brain structures. But it can survive physical death, the theory holds, and waits in God's presence until the resurrection.

The long-continuing discussion about abortion has at times wrangled over the issue of when a soul sup-posedly enters the developing embryo—at conception or sometime later, perhaps at the "quickening." Or as increasing evidence suggests, is the human personality a product of the developing brain?

Some Christians have offered as evidence for a be-lief in a soul distinct from the body the fact that God created a physical body for the preexisting Son of God (Hebrews 10:5). But it is dangerous and pure specula-tion to draw parallels between the incarnation of Christ and the physical existence of human beings.

Others have claimed that it is possible for a body

to exist without a soul. Some years ago an evangelical writer sought to combine Christian evangelistic witness with the popular literary genre of the mystery story. He authored a series of detective novels with strong religious themes. One plot concerned a mad scientist who cloned human beings. Because they were not born the normal way, they lacked souls, and demons took over the uninhabited bodies.

More recently, in published articles on the biology and ethics of human cloning, the authors have had to deal with the question of whether such clones would or would not have souls. Most experts have agreed that a cloned human being would have a soul.

The concept of the soul is a religious one. Most Christians would assume that the Bible teaches that we have a soul separate from the body. All of the questions we have examined derive from the assumption that the soul is either independent of the body or a divisible part of the human personality. But what does Scripture actually say? What did God create in the beginning?

Soul in the Old Testament

The King James Version translation of Genesis 2:7 declares that when God formed man from the ground and breathed the breath of life into him, he became a "living soul."[22] Other modern translations render the Hebrew phrase here, *nephesh chayyah,* as "living being." The basic meaning of *nephesh,* the word usually thought of as referring to the soul, is "throat" (the site of the breath). *Nephesh* appears 755 times in the Old Testament. Let us look at some of the ways that Scripture uses the word to see how the Bible writers understood it.

First, the word not only indicates human beings but also all living animals. For example, it can be translated in the sense of "creature" in Genesis 1:21, 24; 2:19; 9:10, 12, 15, 16; and in Leviticus 11:46. In Leviticus 24:18 it refers to an animal and to a fish in Isaiah 19:10, KJV. Thus animals are souls as well as human beings. While science has not yet cloned human beings, it has done so in the case of animals. And the cloned animals have behaved just like their normal counterparts. Dolly the sheep did not differ from other members of her species.

When applied to human beings, *nephesh* can substitute for a personal pronoun, such as in Numbers 23:10, Judges 16:30, and 1 Kings 20:32. In the latter passage, "let my soul live" simply means "let *me* live." The *nephesh* has all the characteristics of a full and normal human being. A *nephesh* can hunger and thirst (Deuteronomy 12:15, 20f.; 14:26; 1 Samuel 2:16; Psalm 107:5, 9; Proverbs 6:30). Also, it can desire as possessions such physical objects as livestock and wine (Deuteronomy 14:26), a sexual relationship (Genesis 34:3, 8; Song of Solomon 3:1-4), another person's presence (1 Samuel 18:1, 3), and, in the case of a barren woman, a child (1 Samuel 1:15).

Usually we think of a soul in the context of spiritual things, and *nephesh* does have religious interests and drives (Psalm 19:8; 23:3; 65:6; 131:2; Jeremiah 31:25). Besides the spiritual aspect of life, *nephesh* may indicate the human seat of emotions and experiences. It may be sad (Deuteronomy 28:65; Psalm 42:6; 119:28), may grieve (Job 30:25), may feel pain (Psalm 13:2), or may weep (Jeremiah 13:17). Whatever we think a human being can do, so can the *nephesh*. Life may stress it

(Genesis 42:21), make it bitter (Job 3:20; 7:10; Isaiah 38:15), or otherwise trouble it (Isaiah 15:4). A *nephesh* may display any human emotion, such as hate (2 Samuel 5:8; Psalm 11:5) or rejoicing (Psalm 35:9; Isaiah 61:10). One can cheer the *nephesh* (Psalm 86:4; 94:19). Furthermore, it may bless the Lord (Psalm 103:1, 22; 104:1, 35) or may love (1 Samuel 18:1, 3; Song of Solomon 1:7; 3:1, 4). And *nephesh* may indicate thought and memory (Psalm 103:2; Lamentations 3:20). Thus a *nephesh* and a human being are generally interchangeable in the Old Testament.

Further, the Old Testament sees the *nephesh* as so fundamental to being alive that Deuteronomy 12:23 states that "the blood is the life [*nephesh*]." When used this way, *nephesh* can be poured out (Isaiah 53:12; Lamentations 2:12), taken by God (Job 27:8), sought by others (Proverbs 29:10), or forfeited (Habakkuk 2:10)—all descriptions of life itself. God may save or redeem a *nephesh* (Psalm 116:4; 2 Samuel 4:9; Psalm 34:22; 72:14) or deliver it (Psalm 55:18; 116:8), including from the grave itself (Psalm 49:15).

Occasionally Scripture will use *nephesh* with "heart" and "strength," seeming to suggest to today's reader that *nephesh* is a different part of the person. But that is to project modern popular usage into the word "soul." Deuteronomy 6:5, for example, employs the terms together to stress that people should devote all of themselves to God.

Ecclesiastes 12:7 says that at death "the dust returns to the earth as it was, and the breath returns to God who gave it." Some have used the verse to support the idea that when we die the soul instantly goes to God, while the body once more becomes dust of the ground. But Ralph L. Smith observes that the "passage may not be saying anything other than death is the result of God's withdrawal of His 'spirit' or 'life-force' from a person."[23] He quotes W. H. Schmidt and A. B. Davidson, who also see death as the point when God's "vitality" or "life-force" departs from a human being.[24]

Roland E. Murphy says that "this is a picture of dissolution, not of immortality, as if there was a *reditus animae ad Deum,* 'the return of the soul to God.' There is no question of the 'soul' here, but of the life-breath, a totally different category of thought."[25]

The *nephesh* is not just part of a person, but it is the person themself. The word can refer to the physical aspect of life, the emotions, spiritual language, or any other facet of the consciousness. The biblical writer would even use *nephesh* to indicate what we would call a human statistic (Genesis 46:26, 27, KJV). C. M. Robeck, Jr., in his article on the soul in the *International Standard Bible Encyclopedia,* observes that the death of a *nephesh* means a loss of personhood. Thus it is not what Adam *had,* but what he *was.*[26]

After surveying how Scripture uses *nephesh,* Lawrence W. Richards concludes that "'soul' in the OT . . . does not indicate some immaterial part of human beings that continues after death. *Nepeš* essentially means life as it is uniquely experienced by personal beings."[27]

Soul in the New Testament

The New Testament counterpart to the Hebrew word *nephesh* is the Greek word *psyché.* The Greek translation of the Old Testament (the Septuagint) employs *psyché* in the same wide range of usages,[28] and it carries most of the same basic meanings, as we see from the fact that the Septuagint had *psyché* translate *nephesh*. Like *nephesh, psyché* can refer even to a nonhuman living organism, as in the case of the sea creatures of Revelation 8:9; 16:3. Again, as with the Old Testament, the New Testament has Adam becoming a "living being" (1 Corinthians 15:45). Also paralleling Old Testament practice, New Testament listings of people can speak of them as individual souls (Acts 2:41; 7:14). *Psyché* can substitute for a personal pronoun as in Luke 12:19.

Again echoing *nephesh, psyché* can stand for the inner life or personhood. That personhood is priceless (Matthew 16:26; Mark 8:37). It can be purified through obedience to truth (1 Peter 1:22; 3 John 2) and through ministry to others (Acts 14:22). False teachers can deceive "unsteady souls" (2 Peter 2:14; cf. Acts 15:24), or as we would say today, "unstable personalities." To help a "soul" to see the error of their ways is to save that "soul" or person (James 5:20). Clinging to God's covenant promises will provide believers with "a sure and steadfast anchor of the soul" (Hebrews 6:19). It is the whole personality that gains security and steadiness.

The New Testament urges us to entrust our "souls," our personhoods or whole beings, to the protection of a faithful Creator (1 Peter 4:19). And those who maintain their faith despite suffering will keep their souls (Hebrews 10:39); that is, they will not be lost. If you substitute "personhood" for "soul" in these passages they will still make the same sense.

When compared to the Old Testament, the New Testament does contain some elements that at first glance might appear puzzling. Paul, for example, prays that his readers' "spirit and soul and body [may] be kept sound and blameless at the coming of our Lord Jesus Christ" (1 Thessalonians 5:23). "The Pauline reference to spirit, soul, and body . . . has led to extended debate over the significance of these terms. Earlier students of Pauline anthropology tended to interpret the *psyché* in terms of a Greek psychological dualism between body and soul. More recent scholars have come to view these terms in a more Hebraic fashion, recognizing them as different perspectives on a single human reality."[29]

Charles Sherlock comments on this passage that "the vocabulary here is certainly 'tripartite'—body, soul, spirit—but that the stress is on the sanctification of the *whole* person, and that in the future coming of Christ. In popular thought, the point of making a sharp distinction between body and soul is the assertion that the body does not survive death, and people sense that something else must do so. The text . . . teaches that every aspect of being human is to be kept for the coming of Christ, which contradicts the reason for dividing up human beings. Paul is free to speak of being human from different aspects, but avoids any obscuring of the unitary reality we find in Christ, seeing it as headed toward greater fulfillment in Christ, not division."[30]

In 1 Corinthians 5:4, 5 Paul speaks of church leaders disciplining members by turning them over to Satan for the destruction of the flesh so the spirit can be saved. But the apostle employs the term "flesh" in a number of ways in his writings.[31] One of them is as a symbol for rebellious human nature, the perspective employed here.[32] Paul wants the church to allow a member's sinful human nature to be purged through suffering that he hopes will lead to repentance and salvation. He is not contrasting physical nature with immaterial spirit. Such examples instruct us that we must always carefully examine a text to see how in each instance the biblical authors use particular words and images.

Hebrews 4:12 also seems to speak of a division of soul and body: "Indeed, the word of God is living and active, sharper than any two-edged sword, piercing until it divides soul from spirit, joints from marrow; it is able to judge the thoughts and intentions of the heart." Sherlock observes that "the text is even clearer about the issues: if a strict division between body and soul is held, so must a divide be made between joints and marrow! The obvious point is that the gospel of Christ finds its way to the very core of our being, our 'heart.' In order to speak of the gospel's effective work in sinners the vocabulary of division is used. But there is no thought of it reflecting our actual nature. It is sin which divides us from God, and brings the sense of division within each one of us. It is thus not our material nature as such, but that nature as corrupted, which brings about the common distinction between body, soul, mind, or spirit."[33]

Each human being is an indivisible whole. "In the Bible, a person is a unity. Body and soul or spirit are not opposite terms, but rather terms that supplement one another to describe aspects of the whole person."[34] The biblical evidence overwhelmingly supports what science has also been telling us: We are all inseparable mind/body units. The body with its brain is not a shell to house the soul—it is a constituent part of the soul.

God Alone Has Immortality

Besides ruling out the idea that a soul can exist independently of a body,[35] Scripture also denies immortality to human beings. Only God is immortal. First Timothy 6:15, 16 states that God is "the blessed and only Sovereign, the King of kings and Lord of Lords. . . . It is he alone who has immortality." Thus God alone has inherent eternal existence that is not derived from any other source.

The Old Testament does not have a term for immortality. The nearest it comes to one is the single use of *al-mawet* ("no death") in Proverbs 12:28. In the New Testament only Paul uses the Greek nouns *athanasia* ("deathlessness") and *aphtharsia* ("incorruptibility"), and he employs them to describe the "spiritual," or resurrection body, never the "soul." Thus he never mentions the word "soul" in connection with eternal life.[36] The New Testament defines human "immortality" "as the immunity from decay and death that results from sharing the divine life of the resurrected state."[37] That immunity is a gift from God, not something that we inherently possess.

All created beings have only derived life, because it is God "who gives life to all things" (1 Timothy 6:13). It is not a part of their natural makeup. God did not create them to be eternally self-existing. Otherwise, they would have had no need to eat from the "tree of life" (Genesis 2:9; 3:22). Adam and Eve lost their opportunity for eternal life. Jesus died on the cross to allow us to have access to it again. But even then the gift of life has stipulations. Romans 2:7 says that "those who by patiently doing good seek for glory and honor *and immortality,* he will give eternal life." Paul later adds, "The wages of sin is death, but the free gift of God is eternal life in Christ Jesus our Lord" (Roman 6:23).

As we said, God did not create human beings with inherent immortality, nor do we have it now. It is a future experience, one that we wait to receive at the Second Coming. And not everyone will obtain it then—only those who have placed themselves in Christ (1 Corinthians 15:23, 49, 53f.; 2 Peter 1:4). God will have to make those who accept Him capable of never dying. "Man's immortality is not essential [of his nature or essence] or intrinsic, but derived or extrinsic. The acquisition of immortality is a privilege reserved for the righteous rather than the prerogative of all mankind."[38]

---

[1] His skull and the tamping rod are on display at the Countway Library of Medicine in Boston, Massachusetts.

[2] Judith Hooper and Dick Teresi, *The 3-pound Universe* (New York: Macmillan Pub. Co., 1986), p. 39; Oliver Sacks, *An Anthropologist on Mars: Seven Paradoxical Tales* (New York: Alfred A. Knopf, 1995), pp. 59-61; Antonio P. Damasio, Descartes' *Error: Emotion, Reason, and the Human Brain* (New York: Grosset Putnam, 1994), pp. 3-33; John Fleischman, *Phineas Gage: A Gruesome But True Story About Brain Science* (Boston: Houghton Mifflin Company, 2002).

[3] Jeneen Interlandi, "Mysteries of Memory," *Newsweek*, Sept. 22, 2008, p. 64.

[4] http://news.yahoo.com/s/hsn/20081029/hl_hsn/scientistsidentifybrainshatecircuit/.

[5] Bonne Steffen, "Loving a Perfect Stranger," *Christian Reader,* November/December 1997, pp. 24-33.

[6] Sacks, pp. 42-76.

[7] Sacks, *The Man Who Mistook His Wife for a Hat and Other Clinical Tales* (New York: Harper and Row, 1987), pp. 23-42. The pioneer case of the loss of the ability to make new memories was that of a

patient called M. M. See Philip J. Hilts, *Memory's Ghost: The Strange Tale of Mr. M. and the Nature of Memory.*

[8] Alan Mozes, "Scientists Erase Specific Memories in Mice," http://news.yahoo.com/s/hsn/20081022/hl_scientistserasespecificmemoriesinmice.

[9] Michael D. Lemonick, "Glimpses of the Mind," *Time,* July 17, 1995, pp. 48, 49.

[10] Sharon Begley, "One Pill Makes You Larger, and One Pill Makes You Smaller . . ." *Newsweek,* Feb. 7, 1994, p. 39.

[11] Alice Park, "Why We Take Risks—It's the Dopamine," http://news.yahoo.com/s/time/200081231/hl_time/08599186910600.

[12] "For the Obsessed, the Mind Can Fix the Brain," *Newsweek,* Feb. 26, 1996, p. 60.

[13] Josie Glausiusz, "The Chemistry of Obsession," *Discover,* June 1996, p. 36. For more recent research on OCD, see Norman Doidge, *The Brain That Changes Itself: Stories of Personal Triumph From the Frontiers of Brain Science* (New York: Penguin Books, 2007), pp. 164–176.

[14] Candace Pert, *Molecules of Emotion* (New York: Scribner Books, 1997).

[15] Athena Andreadis, *To Seek Out New Life: The Biology of Star Trek* (New York: Crown, 1998).

[16] Michel Craig Miller, "Sad Brain, Happy Brain," *Newsweek* (Sept. 22, 2008), p. 51.

[17] *Ibid.,* p. 52.

[18] Hooper and Teresi, pp. 218–234.

[19] Howard Dully had such an operation at the age of 12. Fortunately for him, he was young enough that his still developing brain was able to compensate for much of the damage, showing another of the amazing powers of the human brain. See Howard Dully with Charles Fleming, *My Lobotomy* (New York: Three Rivers Press, 2008).

[20] Carl Zimmer, "Could inner zombie be controlling your brain? Evidence suggests self-aware part of our brains isn't always in charge," http://www.msnbc.com/id/26742742/.

[21] Steven Pinker, *How the Mind Works* (New York: W. W. Norton and Company, 1997), p. 64.

[22] That is, after God put the breath of life in him, "Adam is living clay as opposed to ordinary clay" (Paul J. Achtemeier, ed., *HarperCollins Bible Dictionary* [San Francisco: Harper San Francisco, 1996], p. 1055).

[23] Ralph L. Smith, *Old Testament Theology: Its History, Method, and*

Message (Nashville: Broadman & Holman Publishers, 1993), p. 377.

[24] *Ibid.*

[25] Roland E. Murphy, *Ecclesiastes, Word Biblical Commentary* (Dallas: Word Books, 1992), vol. 23A, p. 120.

[26] Geoffrey W. Bromiley, ed., *The International Standard Biblical Encyclopedia* (Grand Rapids: William B. Eerdmans, 1982), vol. 4, p. 588.

[27] Lawrence W. Richards, *New International Encyclopedia of Bible Words* (Grand Rapids: Zondervan, 1991), p. 576.

[28] Ralph B. Laurin tries to argue in his article on the soul in *Baker's Dictionary of Theology* that the *psychē* is a spiritual entity that exists apart from the body ([Grand Rapids: Baker Book House, 1960], pp. 491, 492). He does acknowledge, though, that the *nephesh* is not an autonomous spiritual entity, and that to Hebrew thought a human being was not a "body" and a "soul," "but rather a 'body-soul,' a unit of vital power" (p. 492).

[29] *International Standard Bible Encyclopedia*, vol. 4, p. 588.

[30] C. Sherlock, *The Doctrine of Humanity* (Downers Grove, Ill.: InterVarsity Press, 1996), p. 218.

[31] See *Dictionary of Paul and His Letters*, eds. Gerald F. Hawthorne, Ralph P. Martin, and Daniel G. Reid (Downers Grove, Ill.: Inter-Varsity Press, 1993), pp. 303-305.

[32] *Ibid.*, p. 305.

[33] Sherlock, p. 218.

[34] "Such a holistic image of a person is maintained also in the New Testament even over against the Greek culture, which, since Plato, sharply separated body and soul with an analytical existence and which saw the soul as the valuable, immortal part of human beings" (*ibid.*).

[35] Christian Wolf states that "according to the Bible, a human being exists as a whole unit and remains also as a whole person in the hand of God after death. A person is not at any time viewed as a bodiless soul" (*ibid.*, pp. 1295, 1296).

[36] T. C. Butler, ed., *Holman Bible Dictionary* (Nashville: Holman Bible Publishers, 1991), p. 1295.

[37] *International Standard Bible Dictionary*, vol. 2, p. 809.

[38] I*bid.*, p. 810.

CHAPTER 4

DRAWN BY THE LIGHT

Ashley was aware of nothing once the anesthetic took effect until she suddenly realized that she was staring up at the ceiling.[1] But instead of lying in a bed she felt as though she were hovering near the ceiling itself, gazing at herself stretched out on the operating table. Surgeons, nurses, and other medical staff clustered around her. Somehow she sensed that something had gone horribly wrong.

A respirator hissed off to one side. Physicians barked orders at the nurses. As the minutes passed and the medical team worked on her, oblivious to her "presence" suspended just below the ceiling of the operating room, Ashley felt herself rise through where the ceiling had been into the dark sky. She drifted steadily higher. Noticing a distant source of light, she started toward it. The glow intensified until it dominated everything else.

Suddenly she sensed forms standing in the light. The light seemed to radiate from their faces, and no matter how bright it got, it did not blind her. To Ashley's surprise, she realized that she knew who some of the beings were. She recognized relatives and friends who had died years before.

Overwhelming joy flooded through her. Then one of the beings sadly shook its head. "It's not time yet,

Ashley. You must go back for a while." Then, in what seemed just moments later, she found herself lying in the recovery room.

Near-Death Experiences

What happened to Ashley is not that unusual. People who have nearly died in accidents, from heart attacks, or on the operating table but were later revived often have what have come to be called near-death experiences (NDEs). They follow consistent patterns: floating free from the body, traveling down a tunnel to a light, meeting dead friends and relatives, and feeling a great sense of peace and bliss. At first only a few physicians were aware of NDEs. The people who had experienced them were reluctant to talk about them, lest others think they were crazy. Then researchers began to write about the phenomenon. Raymond Moody, M.D., did a pioneering study on NDEs in his *Life After Life* (Atlanta: Mockingbird Books, 1975). More books on them flooded bookstores, and special television features appeared on educational channels. Research projects explored them, and journals ranging from standard medical periodicals to specific publications such as *Anabiosis—The Journal for Near-Death Studies* described the findings.

One Gallup poll estimated that one in 20—5 percent—of the American population reported having an NDE.[2] Studies indicate that they appear across a wide range of cultures, religions, and countries. Few would any longer deny that NDEs are real. The question now is What do they mean?

Many see them as confirmation of life after death. Some NDE researchers have suggested that the soul might continue on forever after the body dies, because, according to physics energy can neither be created nor destroyed. But order and information can perish, because of the universal law of entropy. We can broadcast radio or television signals that contain the data for sound or pictures, but electromagnetic waves in time become weaker and weaker until they for all practical purposes vanish. They have no way of preserving themselves, let alone be self-aware and create new data. And the human personality is an unbelievably more complex system of such order and data than an electronic broadcast.

Energy may be indestructible, but life is not. There is a vast difference between, for example, an electrical current flowing straight from a battery or generating plant and one transmitting the music of Handel from a CD or a movie from a DVD. The first is just raw unformed energy while the other contains information. Music and video possess complex information and demand a stable or self-sustaining storage device such as a computer chip to preserve it. The human brain is also a self-sustaining storage system. Apart from the mind of God Himself, it is the most complex information storage device known to humanity.

If the human personality is the sum total of all the order and data contained in the neural structures of the brain, when those neurons die and decompose, the personality is gone. The electrochemical energy that once resided in the brain cells will still exist, but it has no organization or structure. It is just amorphous energy.

NDEs can powerfully affect those who experience them. Often people seem changed by them. Afterward life seems more precious, while the fear of dying eases or vanishes. Sometimes those who have gone through them want to help others, or they seek to share the comfort and faith they now feel. But does that mean they really are portals into the afterlife?

Seeing and Hearing May Not Equal Believing

A semi crushed Don Piper's car and mangled his body. The rescue team had to either send him straight to a hospital or declare him dead before they could move the body. Seeing Piper's condition, they pronounced him dead.

Ninety minutes later a minister prayed over Piper, and he revived. He told others that during those 90 minutes he had found himself standing before the gate of heaven. As he waited there he heard endless music coming from the city that convinced him that he was in heaven. Some of the songs were familiar religious hymns, but most of it he had never heard before at all. Piper sang along with the many choirs inside the city.

The beauty around him was overwhelming. Much of what he saw reflected the imagery of the book of Revelation. The gate of heaven was iridescent like a pearl, and the streets were paved with gold bricks. But when he approached the heavenly gate he suddenly awakened.[3]

The two things that stuck out in Piper's mind were the amazing beauty of what he saw and the fantastic music that he heard. But as wonderful as it all was, it did not offer conclusive proof that he actually went to heaven. Brain studies have revealed that perhaps most human beings have the spontaneous capacity to make music. A wide variety of conditions can cause musical hallucinations.[4] The trauma of the accident may simply have triggered Piper's brain's innate ability to create such music. And the beauty of what he saw may have inspired him but it may have been nothing more than the construct of his own brain using biblical imagery as a starting point.

For a few, however, NDEs have been a nightmare. Those who had them thought that they had entered hell or some other place of punishment after death. Such individuals find themselves driven to transform their lives and to warn others to change theirs also. A few individuals have had both heaven-like and hell-like NDEs together. And some less traditionally religious researchers, such as Kenneth Ring, have suggested that NDEs are an evolutionary development leading to a new global consciousness.[5]

Many of those who have had NDEs explain them as the soul leaving the body, but most researchers have attempted to find physiological causes. A number of psychoactive drugs, certain gases, and a lack of oxygen will produce reactions that mimic some of the characteristics of NDEs. Training exercises for pilots assigned to high-speed jet aircraft subject the aviators to high g-forces. The g-forces restrict the flow of blood to certain areas of the brain. The visual center becomes activated, producing the tunnel of light phenomenon. Then memories of people can come flooding into the consciousness.

The sensation of leaving the body was the most puzzling aspect of NDEs. One day Melvin Morse happened to discuss NDEs with Art Ward, former chairperson of neurosurgery at the University of Washington. Ward had heard some of his patients describe them. He also remembered some research conducted by Wilder Penfield, considered by many to be the father of neurosurgery and the discoverer of much of the contemporary understanding of how the brain functions. Penfield had stimulated a certain area of the brain with an electric probe. When Penfield touched one part, the patient felt as if he were leaving the body. Stimulating a nearby region produced the sensation of zooming up a tunnel.

When Morse and his team of NDE researchers examined the surgeon's work, they found buried in a 40-year-old textbook references to patients on the operating table who when Penfield touched their brains with the electric probe would say "I am leaving my body now" or "I'm half in and half out."

Penfield had been mapping the Sylvian fissure in the right temporal lobe above the right ear. As he touched areas around the fissure "patients frequently had the experience of 'seeing God,' hearing beautiful music, seeing dead friends and relatives, and even having a panoramic life review."[6] Another group of researchers in Chile confirmed the same area of the brain as producing NDE-like phenomena.[7]

A Swiss patient had a neural stimulator implanted in his brain in a desperate attempt to stop a debilitating condition of tinnitus (ringing of the ears). Each time the device was turned on to block the tinnitus, however, he felt as if he were floating outside his body. Positron emission tomography (PET) scans of his brain indicated that the stimulator was activating the right angular-supramarginal gyrus and superior temporal gyrus areas of the brain.[8]

Researchers have discovered other ways to induce the sensation of being outside the body without the aid of electrical stimulation of the brain or the use of drugs. One of them involves the use of virtual-reality goggles that trick the test subjects into thinking that their bodies are in different places than they actually are. Such experiments seek to understand body perception in the brain.[9] Another study suggests that people with different sleep cycles are more likely to have NDEs. For them things normally experienced during sleep will linger over into wakefulness. They will wake up but still feel paralyzed or hear sounds that others do not.[10]

NDE-type phenomena seem to have a variety of causes, and this fact alone questions their validity as evidence of an afterlife.

The Body-Mind Connection

We human beings actually experience the world around us only in our brains. We do not see with our eyes, hear with our ears, or taste with our tongues in the way that we think we do. Instead, the sensory impressions go to the brain, where its various areas process, interpret, and perceive the data. The sensory organs themselves may work perfectly, but if the brain does not have the neural circuitry to process the impulses coming through the nerves from them, we perceive nothing. Thus the baby born with cataracts that do not get removed in time or the adult who has a vision problem that can be corrected through surgery after a lifetime of blindness will still not be able to see because the brain lacks the ability to process the sensory information. And even if we do have the necessary circuitry, anything that affects its functioning will alter how our brains interpret that sensory information.

Our awareness of our bodies also takes place in our brains. Scientific research keeps revealing additional ways how the brain's perception of the body itself not only works but can be altered. Amputees often experience "phantom limb" phenomenon. In it the brain still "feels" a limb that is no longer there. The brain seems to have a map of the body programmed into it, one that still "re-members" the lost limb and can still receive nerve impulses from its stump. As a result the brain interprets those impulses as coming from the full body part. Often the phantom pain seems as if the lost limb is stuck in an uncomfortable position (frequently the position the limb was in when an accident or explosion destroyed it), and painkillers do not seem to help block it.

Physicians treating amputees caused by roadside bombs in Iraq and Afghanistan have had to deal with this problem. Using a box with a system of mirrors that create the illusion that the missing limb is still present, the patient "moves" the limb in the image until it is in a more comfortable position. The pain then begins to disappear for many of the amputees. Apparently the patient is reprogramming the mental map or image of the missing limb in the brain itself. The Walter Reed Army Medical Center adopted the procedure as routine care for such injuries.[11]

The brain can even experience a limb that never existed in the first place. Ronald Melzack, of McGill University in Montreal, Canada, found that people born without a limb can sometimes feel it as if it were there. Seventy-six of the 125 people he studied had lacked a limb since birth. Fifteen reported feeling a limb they had never possessed. One woman had her phantom arm reach out to stop a cupboard door from slamming and to catch a falling egg. A 14-year-old boy with no right arm below the elbow could feel the missing limb when it rained. He also dreamed that he had two hands. An 11-year-old girl who lacked the left arm below the elbow experienced pain in her "fingers" when she bumped her funny bone.

"These findings," says Melzack, suggest that "the body we perceive is in large part built into our brain—it's not entirely learned. In fact, you do not need the body to feel the body." He thinks that a network of neurons forms in the embryonic brain to link the somatosensory thalamus and cortex (regions that enable us to sense the location of our limbs), the limbic system, which is involved in feeling pain and pleasure, and the association cortex, which helps us learn from our experiences. These connections prepare the embryonic brain to respond to body parts that do not always form. "Even if we are missing a part of the body, the brain is still able to generate the perception of the part."[12]

Scientific evidence thus increasingly demonstrates that we actually experience the external world inside our brains, not where it may seem to us.[13] Once again, we note that anything that affects the brain can modify or even distort our perception of external reality. We may even think that we are experiencing something that is not really happening. All these findings caution us to question the credibility of NDEs for "proving" either a detachable and independent soul or for giving us any valid insight into the nature of a possible afterlife.

Mysterious Knowledge

Although Melvin Morse did locate an area of the brain that made a person feel as if they were leaving the physical body, he still believed that *something* had departed from it. He struggled to explain cases of NDE in which the person reported things that Morse felt they could not otherwise possibly know.

While fishing from a bridge, 8-year-old Jimmy fell and hit his head on a rock in the water. The boy floated facedown for at least five minutes before a police officer pulled him out. Jimmy had no pulse and had stopped breathing. The officer performed CPR for 30 minutes before the Medivac helicopter reached the accident site. The paramedics pronounced the boy dead before the helicopter started for the hospital. But Jimmy lived and came out of his coma two days later.

He described to his doctor the rescue in great detail, including the police officer's name, the length of time before the helicopter arrived, and the various life-saving procedures used on him both during the flight and at the hospital. Jimmy said that he had been observing everything from outside his body.

Morse cited a number of other such cases in which NDE individuals could report with great accuracy the events that had happened when they were unconscious. It convinced him that the area of the brain around the Sylvian fissure was a "circuit board" that enabled the consciousness to depart the physical body.

How can unconscious persons possibly know what is going around them? The answer has two aspects. We will look at the first, a natural explanation, in this chapter and the second, a supernatural one, in the next.

Repeated experience has taught medical researchers that just because people are not conscious does not mean that they are unaware of their surroundings. Patients who recover from deep comas often relate in great detail what took place while they were unconscious. Hearing is perhaps the last sense to stop functioning before death.

Medical schools and chaplaincy programs now teach medical staff and clergy to be extremely careful what they say around comatose patients. Negative comments about prognosis can cause some patients to give up their struggle for life and die prematurely. On the other hand, unconscious surgery patients who had the anesthesiologist whisper "You will get well soon" in their ears left the hospital an average of two days sooner than a control group that had not received such encouragement.

Complications can often result from what patients overhear while unconscious. One man whose wife was not expected to live took the woman with whom he had been having an affair along with him to the hospital. As they stood beside the wife's bed, they discussed plans for their marriage as soon as the wife died. The comatose wife heard them, and when she regained consciousness she confronted the husband about his affair.

A friend of the author's wife had an extreme reaction to anesthetics. During one operation the anesthetic had stopped her heartbeat. The next time she had to undergo an operation she carefully explained the problem beforehand to the attending physician. He dismissed her concern, figuring she was a chronic worrier. But as the operation progressed, even though she was unconscious, the woman could hear the surgical team discussing the fact that her heart had once again quit beating.

Unconscious people can pick up many clues from conversation and other sounds about what is taking place around them. Their minds fill in the details, creating vivid images as the brain does while dreaming. As for being aware of events taking place some distance away or otherwise beyond a person's ability to know about, as some cases of NDE seem to suggest, we will explore that in the next chapter.

But before we do that we must remind ourselves of a fundamental reality. Those who argue that NDEs represent the soul's temporary visit to the afterlife must face the fact that science cannot prove that the individuals really died. They may have only dropped to an extremely low level of biological and neurological activity. The victims came close to the edge of death, but we cannot tell if they actually passed beyond it. If scientists could revive a decayed brain that then exhibited no negative changes in personality or memory, we would have striking evidence. But for now we cannot demonstrate that the brains of those experiencing NDEs actually cease all functioning, that its incredibly complex structure has degraded beyond any possibility of spontaneous recovery. We must regard as unproven the argument that NDEs allow souls to take a peek into the afterworld.

---

[1] Based on a composite of many such reported incidents.

[2] George Gallup, Jr., *Adventures in Immortality* (New York: Mc-Graw Hill, 1982).

³ Don Piper with Cecil Murphey, *90 Minutes in Heaven* (Grand Rapids: Revell, 2004). The book has sold several million copies.

⁴ Oliver Sacks, Musicophilia: *Tales of Music and the Brain,* rev. and expanded. (New York: Vintage, 2008), pp. 54-92; John J. Pilch, "Music and Trance," in *Music and Altered States: Consciousness, Transcendence, Therapy and Addiction* (London: Jessica Kingsley Publishers, 2006), pp. 38-50.

⁵ Kenneth Ring, *Heading Toward Omega: In Search of the Meaning of the Near-Death Experience* (New York: William Morrow, 1985).

⁶ Melvin Morse and Paul Perry, *Closer to the Light: Learning From the Near-Death Experiences* of Children (New York: Ivy Books, 1990), pp. 118, 119. Penfield's textbook (with Theodore Rasmussen) would be *The Cerebral Cortex of Man* (New York: Macmillan, 1950).

⁷ *Ibid.,* p. 125.

⁸ Dirk De Ridder et al, "Visualizing Out-of-Body Experiences in the Brain," *New England Journal of Medicine* 357(2007): 1829-1833.

⁹ Dave Mosher, "Scientists simulate out-of-body experiences: virtual-reality experiments give subjects that disembodied feeling," http://www.msnbc.msn.com/id/20411858/from/RS.4/.

¹⁰ Shankar Vedantam, "Near-Death Experiences Linked to Sleep Cycles," Washington *Post,* Apr. 11, 2006.

¹¹ Maia Szalavitz, "Phantom Pain Treated With 'Mirror Therapy,'" http://health.msn.com/health-topics/pain-management/articlepage.aspx?cp-documentid+100215594>1=31035.

¹² "Phantom Limbs," *Discover,* February 1998, p. 20.

¹³ For more fascinating insights into how the human brain works, see V. S. Ramachandran and Sandra Blakeslee, *Phantoms in the Brain: Human Nature and the Architecture of the Mind* (London: Harper Perennial, 2005); V. S. Ramachandran, *A Brief Tour of Human Consciousness: From Impostor Poodles to Purple Numbers* (New York: Pi Press, 2004).

CHAPTER 5

SUPERNATURAL DECEPTION

When Sir Arthur Conan Doyle created the character of Sherlock Holmes, the detective who approached every situation with disciplined powers of observation and careful deduction, he based many of Holmes's abilities on his own remarkable talents of analytical observation and reasoning. In the stories the author always had the private investigator approach his cases through logic and examination.

Doyle began two Holmes stories—"The Adventure of the Dancing Men" and "The Adventure of the Cardboard Box" with nearly identical scenes. The detective startles his friend Dr. Watson by announcing what his longtime chronicler had just been thinking. Naturally Watson is amazed. Holmes then explains that by combining his knowledge of the doctor's habits, looking for physical clues (such as chalk dust on Watson's fingers), and watching as the friend gazed at a portrait and other objects about the room, the detective could follow what must be Watson's thought processes. The master investigator didn't need to be psychic to guess what his friend must be thinking. He rejected anything that smacked of the supernatural.

Unfortunately, Doyle forgot to follow his literary character's practice in his own later life. All throughout his life Doyle had been fascinated by paranormal forces and abilities such as telepathy and with the relation of the mind to the soul. His father was an alcoholic and troubled with mental illness. Doyle sought ways to relate the father's behavior with the soul he could not conceive of as causing such actions. For a time his medical studies with their emphasis on rationalism made him skeptical of much of the occult and paranormal even though it intrigued him. Then, shortly after he created his fictional and ultra-logical detective, Doyle discovered spiritualism. Even then he was still cautious toward it. But he began to regard it as a new form of science, and sought to reconcile it with more traditional forms of science. One wonders how he would have come to view spiritualism if he had been aware of the findings of modern mind/body research.

The incident that prompted him to accept spiritualism whole-heartedly occurred when a medium named Horstead produced an example of "spirit writing" that said Doyle should not read a book by Leigh Hunt entitled *Comic Dramatists of the Restoration*. Arthur had been debating whether or not to read the book but had been put off by what he knew of the lewdness of Restoration plays. He had not told anyone of his feelings, however.[1] Doyle thought that the spirits could read his thoughts, not realizing that his musings could be interpreted by others, whether human or supernatural, just by observing him as he had Sherlock Holmes doing to Dr. Watson. The death of his son during World War I intensified Doyle's obsession with spiritualism. He wrote a two-volume work on the subject and traveled the world defending his new beliefs. Sadly, he did not apply his own reasoning ability to the question of whether there might be fraud in spiritualism on either the human or supernatural levels.

Because he so desperately wanted to believe in spiritualism, he suspended his cautionary reasoning powers to the point that he let himself be deceived by some children. In 1917 Doyle wrote that fairies had been discovered in the English village of Cottingley. Sixteen-year-old Elsie Wright and her 10-year-old cousin, Frances Griffiths took photographs of each other by a wooded stream. In front of them winged spirits danced and played on musical instruments.

Several photography experts who examined the photographs declared that they had not been created by superimposing one image upon another or through re-touching. Doyle joyfully regarded them as proof of supernatural creatures, thus in his mind increasing even further the plausibility of a supernatural afterlife.[2] Eventually media interest in the fairy pictures faded, though it further damaged Doyle's reputation. Not until the early 1980s, when Elsie and Frances were elderly women, did they explain how they had faked the photographs. They copied drawings from a volume entitled *Princess Mary's Gift Book* (ironically, Doyle had published a story called "Bimbashi Joyce" in that very collection), stuck them on hat pins, and photographed themselves with the cutouts positioned in front of them.[3]

In later years Doyle would patiently sit in the woods near his estate with a music box and a camera, hoping to lure fairies out in the open and capture images of them on film.[4] He had long forgotten to listen to the caution and insights of his own literary character and had become credulous to almost anything.

To venture into the realms of spiritualism and other forms of the paranormal is to encounter fraud on either the human or supernatural level. The former can caution us about trusting certain elements of the near-death experience. But before we examine supernatural deception in NDEs, we must look briefly at spiritualism itself.

Seeking Help From Beyond

Human beings have apparently attempted to communicate with the dead since the beginning of human existence. Desperate for any help and guidance they could get in a world in which extinction seemed always just a famine, plague, or war away, the people of the ancient world explored every avenue to the supernatural they could imagine. Besides the gods, they sought aid from the dead. After all, the dead had once been part of the human family and could understand the problems that the living still faced. The dead surely had access to powers that the living might otherwise have trouble enlisting to protect and support them.

The archaeological evidence repeatedly demonstrates that popular religion included regular rituals for the benefit of the dead. Relatives and friends of the deceased assembled at graves and tombs to offer food and drink for the departed. Some ancient tombs had shafts leading into the ground not only to permit offerings to reach the dead but also to serve as a channel for communication with them.

The living considered the dead as still part of the family. They were still responsible for the care and feeding of their ancestors. In Egypt families endowed shrines and priests to maintain regular offerings for the deceased.

Also, they might offer pottery with messages inscribed, requesting help for the birth of a child or for other needs.

Naturally the powerful customs of caring for the dead and invoking their aid attracted the interest of the Israelites. As a result, God had to forbid food offerings to the dead (Deuteronomy 26:14; Psalm 106:28). Deuteronomy 18:9-14 prohibited a number of rituals that sought guidance from the supernatural, including divination, consulting ghosts or spirits, or trying to obtain oracles from the deceased. Exodus 22:18 imposed the death penalty on female sorcerers. Leviticus 19:26, 31 and 20:6, 27 warned against mediums, sorcerers, and other practitioners of the occult.

But consulting with the dead still has a powerful lure to it, as we see in the rise of modern spiritualism. Many trace its origin to the careers of Margaret Fox (1833-1893) and Catherine Fox (1839-1893). In 1848 they reported hearing a series of rappings in their farmhouse near Rochester, New York. They claimed that the sounds were messages from the spirit of a murdered man and that they could communicate with him. The social climate of the period was primed for great interest in such a topic, and their accounts set off a media frenzy.

The heavy casualties of the American Civil War intensified the fascination with spiritualism. Records of the time indicate that the number of spiritists in the United States rose to 7 million by 1863.[5] One spiritist publication, the *Banner of Light,* claimed 10 million adherents after the conflict, having gained 1 million per year for three years. Many felt that the vast numbers of young men and others killed in the war had "passed over" to a land just beyond the living, where they could be called upon to comfort and support the loved ones they had left behind.[6]

Spiritualism received another boost at the end of World War I with its millions of casualties. Grieving people such as Arthur Conan Doyle desperately wanted assurance that their loved ones were not forever lost, and they would grasp at any straw. People long for some hint that death is not the end of existence, or that there is some kind of hope in dealing with the insolvable issues of life. Channeling has become one of the more recent forms of necromancy and spiritualism. Such channelers usually present themselves as the conduit of some powerful individual from the past, often a great warrior or leader from a golden age thousands of years ago. The being speaking through the human agent claims to possess insights that will solve the complicated problems facing modern civilization. If people will just listen and follow the supernatural counsel, it will transform society and lead to a new golden age.

From the biblical perspective, though, any claim to be the spirit or consciousness of a person from the past must be rejected. Human beings have no immortal soul to linger on after the death of the physical body. The dead have ceased to exist and will come back into being only when God restores them to life. Many evangelicals and other Christians correctly reject channeling and other occult practices, seeing it as the work of fallen angels or demons. But by believing in an immortal soul, they are still vulnerable to satanic deception. After all, if people do have an immortal soul that can survive apart from the body, why can it not leave the body and visit heaven or elsewhere for a brief period? How else can one explain some of the unexpected knowledge or abilities that people acquire during NDEs?

Strange Knowledge and Abilities

An incident presented as part of a program about NDEs on the cable Learning Channel told of a medical doctor who had experienced an NDE in a plane crash. Later she had a vision in which she saw a friend's brain surrounded by pus. The physician encouraged her friend to have medical tests on her brain. The tests revealed that the friend was in the early stages of a rare brain infection. With the condition caught so quickly, the friend survived the disease without any neurological damage—something unusual in adult cases of that particular disease.

Here we come to the second aspect of the answer to the mystery of NDEs—the supernatural aspect. Supernatural beings would have known that the friend had contracted the disease, and taking advantage of the NDE, communicated it to the physician without her realizing it. The doctor thought she had, after the incident, psychic abilities that she really did not possess.

Such supernatural agencies—the fallen angels of which Scripture speaks so frequently[7]—as they seek to convince individuals that they really have entered heaven or hell may also be able to trigger sensory impressions in the mind of the traumatized brain. When the persons recover, they are convinced that they have glimpsed the afterlife. And they persuade others about its reality, which is Satan's goal. He is determined to deceive the human race about its true nature.

How could supernatural beings communicate with someone without others being aware of it? We have infinitely more to learn about how the brain works, but at this point some scientific evidence suggests that whether its conscious or subconscious area registers a particular sensory stimulus depends upon its duration. If it is extremely brief, the subconscious might detect it but not the consciousness. For example, you may have had the experience of thinking of someone and then turning around and to your surprise actually seeing the person. The suggestion is that you spotted the person at the subconscious level before they registered on the conscious level. That brief subconscious awareness triggered the thought about them.

Further research may reveal still other ways that the brain becomes aware of the world around us, avenues that supernatural beings can manipulate to deceive the brain when it is under NDE-type conditions. Scripture clearly indicates that evil agencies can influence human beings. And history does teach us that what we recognize as evil (too often after the fact) does sway society. But however such forces affect humanity, it serves Satan's purpose for people to come back from the edge of death convinced that they have seen its other side and that the human race is immortal and cannot perish. He is still trying to convince human beings of his original lie to them—that they will not die. After all, who would want to deny the testimony of someone who has seemingly returned from death? Who would not be thrilled to know that deceased loved ones are happy and safe in some kind of an afterlife? What could be more comforting than the thought that we each have an immortal soul and that bliss awaits it? No wonder so many have peace and assurance after a near-death experience. They think they can face death with confidence—but it is a false assurance. It is trusting in subjective personal experience rather than in the objective revelation of the One who created all life.

Satanic forces will do anything to deceive humans into thinking that they are immortal. My mother had a friend who had received Bible studies on the nature of death and the dead. But the woman mentioned that her dead mother frequently visited her. When reminded that the apparition must be a demon, the friend protested that it had to be her mother. It told her things that no one else could possibly have known. Several years passed before the woman recognized that the being was not really her mother.

In such incidents supernatural beings have access to information that human beings do not. They see what is going on everywhere (even in secret), have thousands of years of experience with human nature, and can put together a highly convincing fraud. Like Arthur Conan Doyle's Sherlock Holmes, the fallen angels can tell much of what we are thinking just from carefully observing us. And they know how to manipulate our minds and emotions and senses.

People who might never think of consulting a medium or attending a séance can still leave themselves open to the potential deception of an NDE message. In Jesus' parable about the rich man and Lazarus (to be discussed in a later chapter), Abraham tells the rich man that the latter's brothers would not listen even if someone did bring a warning from beyond the grave (Luke

16:31). But is that really true? Could NDEs be an exception? After all, didn't God send a message from the afterworld in the Old Testament case of the woman of Endor?

The Woman of Endor

Perhaps the most dramatic account in Scripture of someone attempting to find supernatural help was Saul's visit to the witch, or sorcerer, of Endor. He wanted her to contact the spirit of his former mentor, the prophet Samuel.

Many have seen in the incident evidence that the dead are conscious and can return to the land of the living. Walter J. Kaiser, Jr., claims that "the most prevalent view among orthodox commentators is that there was a genuine appearance of Samuel brought about by God Himself."[8] He believes "that God allowed Samuel's spirit to give Saul one more warning about the evil of his ways."[9]

But does 1 Samuel 28:3-25 really teach that the dead come back from the grave—even to deliver a message from God? Let us look carefully at some of the many clues the biblical author places in his story that help us determine how to interpret it. What is the incident really about?

Saul, the first king of Israel, found his kingdom collapsing about him. He had systematically turned away from God and His prophet, Samuel. Finally the Lord had no choice but to declare through Samuel that He would have to transfer the kingdom to another human ruler (1 Samuel 15:28). Besides the guerrilla warfare Saul waged against his rival David, the Philistines had left their territories along the coast and were over-whelming the hill country of the Israelites. The king was desperate. The prophet had died, and God seemed to have totally turned His back on Saul, even when the king sought His help. The monarch wanted divine guidance, but the usual avenues to the God of Israel remained ominously silent (1 Samuel 28:6).

Finally, feeling that he had no other recourse, Saul, who in obedience to God's law had previously expelled the wizards and sorcerers (verse 3), now turned to one of them. If God would not answer him directly, then perhaps he could get help from his old nemesis through another route. It could be that the king hoped that the dead prophet might be able to change God's mind in the way that non-Israelites thought the dead could intercede for them. But the question persists, If God refused to respond through a living prophet, why would He now do so through a dead one?

The king made a risky journey behind Philistine lines to reach the woman of Endor. When Saul requested that she raise a spirit, she feared a trap (verses 8, 9). In response, Saul vowed by the God who had forbidden sorcery that nothing would happen to her (verse 10). "No reader can miss the irony that Saul was both lawmaker and lawbreaker. Saul swore by the life of Yahweh—again an ironic contrast with the spirits of the dead he wanted to invoke—that no guilt would accrue to the woman because of her actions."[10]

The desperate Saul now specifically asked that she summon Samuel, and she realized who her nocturnal visitor was (verse 12). Interestingly, the king apparently did not see the alleged apparition, and identified what

85

the woman claimed to have called up only by the description of it as an old man wearing a robe, possibly the badge of the prophetic office (verse 14).[11] Significantly, verse 13 announces that the entity summoned by the woman was an *elohim*. A Hebrew word never used for the dead, it normally refers to a supernatural being, either divine or demonic.

The being called "Samuel" demanded to know why Saul had disturbed him. The king explained that he was "in great distress, for the Philistines are warring against me, and God has turned away from me and answers me no more, either by prophets or by dreams; so I have summoned you to tell me what I should do" (verse 15).[12] When the prophet had been alive Saul had refused to heed him. Now he begged "Samuel's" guidance from the grave.

The apparition told Saul that God was fulfilling His earlier prediction against the king, that He had not changed His mind (verses 16, 17). Because Saul did not obey God but went his own way, his fate, that of his sons, and that of what was left of his nation was sealed—death at the hands of the Philistines (verses 18, 19).

In fear the king fell to the ground (verse 20). "Saul, who stood a head taller than all his colleagues (1 Samuel 9:2), now lay stretched out before the prophet to his entire height."[13] He had bowed before something he could not even see.

The king was also weak from not eating (whether from a ritualistic fasting in preparation for the summoning of a spirit or simply because he was too panic-stricken to eat). The woman offered him food, but he at first refused. Finally she and his servants convinced him to eat (verses 21-23), offering him a fatted calf (verse 24). He ate and left (verse 25).[14]

Perhaps we can get another clue here to what the biblical writer was doing in this passage by noticing that earlier Saul's kingdom had begun with a meal provided by a prophet, Samuel (1 Samuel 9). The special portion held back for him may have come from the sacrifice Samuel had offered. Now Saul's kingdom was ending with a meal provided by a false prophetic voice. Although the author does not comment on the nature of the "Samuel" summoned by the woman sorcerer, he does hint at it by creating a reverse image of Saul's rise. Demons can tell the truth if it suits their purpose—as it did in this case. It threw Saul into absolute and hopeless despair. And God can—if He so chooses—allow even a demon to fulfill His will (cf. 1 Kings 22:19-23).

But even more important, we must keep in mind that "the narrative is meant to be taken as the penultimate act of a man who is involved in guilt and who now meets his desserts."[15] The passage is not an exposition of the afterlife, but a dramatic demonstration of where rebellion against God ultimately leads.

The author of 1 Samuel is focused on Saul and his fate. Everything else is extraneous and somewhat irrelevant. "The intention of this story is to emphasize Saul's hopelessness—and to show how low he had sunk, when even a criminal helped to comfort him. For the woman was a criminal, by Saul's own laws. The chapter is certainly not endorsing the activities of mediums; God's guidance is never to be obtained from them."[16]

We need to take seriously what Alexander Heidel, in his comparison of the Old Testament descriptions of the dead with those of Mesopotamian cultures, decided about the Endor story: "I believe that the whole affair was a demonic delusion, reminding of 2 Thessalonians 2:9-12."[17] He concluded that the Old Testament teaches that the dead cannot in any way influence the living.[18] And that would include through NDEs or any other supernatural phenomenon.

[1] Andrew Lycett, *The Man Who Created Sherlock Holmes: The Life and Times of Arthur Conan Doyle* (New York: Free Press, 2007), pp. 139, 140.

[2] His father had also been interested in fairies.

[3] Lycett, pp. 408, 409, 414. To view some of the photographs themselves as well as additional background, see www.museumofhoaxes.com/hoax/Hoaxipedia/Cottingley_Fairies; http://en.wikipedia.org/wiki/Cottingley_Faries; http://fictive.arts.uci.edu/cottingley_faires. The incident inspired the 1997 movie *Fairy Tale: A True Story*. However, the scriptwriters and producers couldn't resist the temptation to introduce fantasy and supernatural elements into the narrative.

[4] Lycett, p. 452.

[5] Barbara Goldsmith, *Other Powers: The Age of Suffrage, Spiritualism, and the Scandalous Victoria Woodhull* (New York: Alfred A. Knopf, 1998), p. 78.

[6] *Ibid.*, p. 139.

[7] See such passages as Ephesians 6:12; Revelation 12:7-9; Romans 8:37-39. Scripture repeatedly warns against getting involved with dangerous supernatural powers, commonly referred to as the occult. See such passages as Deuteronomy 18:10-12; Isaiah 8:19; Leviticus 20:27.

[8] Walter C. Kaiser, Jr., Peter H. Davids, F. F. Bruce, and Manfred T. Brauch, *Hard Sayings of the Bible* (Downers Grove, Ill.: InterVarsity Press, 1996), p. 217.

[9] *Ibid.*, p. 218.

[10] Ralph W. Klein, *1 Samuel, Word Biblical Commentary* (Waco, Tex.: Word Books, 1983), vol. 10, p. 271.

[11] Joyce Baldwin, *1 and 2 Samuel: An Introduction and Commentary* (Leicester, Eng.: InterVarsity Press, 1988), p. 159.

[12] Could there be even more irony lurking in Saul's statement that God no longer answers by a prophet? And is the author giving a clue to one of the meanings of this strange and disturbing episode?

[13] Klein, p. 272.

[14] "He listened to her and to his servants, but he did not listen to the voice of Yahweh" (*ibid.,* p. 273).

[15] Hans Wilhelm Hertzberg, *1 and 2 Samuel: A Commentary* (Philadelphia: Westminster Press, 1964), p. 220.

[16] *New Bible Commentary, 21st Century Edition* (Leicester, Eng.: InterVarsity Press, 1994), p. 319.

[17] A. Heidel, *The Gilgamesh Epic and Old Testament Parallels,* p. 189.

[18] *Ibid.,* p. 206.

CHAPTER 6

DÉJÀ VU ALL OVER AGAIN

(REINCARNATION AND KARMA)

Although he grew up in a Christian home and studied the Bible extensively, the entertainer Willie Nelson became fascinated with the concept of reincarnation.[1] Reincarnation (also called transmigration of souls or metempsychosis) teaches that if the soul can exist apart from the body it should also be able to inhabit other bodies after the death of the first one. Eventually Nelson incorporated his beliefs into a popular song, "Highwayman." It tells of a soul first hung as a bandit, then perishing in an accident during the construction of Boulder Dam, and finally crossing the universe as the pilot of a starship. The song is but one of countless examples of the concept's influence on popular culture.

Reincarnation has an ancient history. The ancient Greeks and a number of primitive peoples have held it. Africans thought that the souls of their kings entered lions, and Irish tradition tells of the rebirth of heroes. In some areas of Asia people assumed that the souls of the dead might go into their crops. Even modern Americans are coming to accept the concept. A recent Harris Poll reveals that 24 percent believe that the soul can occupy one body after another.

But reincarnation's greatest following so far has been among Buddhism, Hinduism, Jainism, Sikhism, and related religions that developed in India. The East Indian religions tie reincarnation to the law of karma. The concept of karma teaches that a person's actions in one life determine the kind of body their soul will enter during the next reincarnation. Those who live good lives will be reborn into a higher state, such as that of a Hindu priest. But those with morally questionable lives will find themselves reborn at a lesser level, perhaps even in an animal such as a dog or insect. The idea has entered Western thought and popular culture. Willie Nelson recorded a song with a refrain about karma. He saw the concept as the answer to a deep question with which he struggled.

Noting the suffering millions who starved to death or perished in massacres, he said, "You wonder why a just and loving God would let things like that happen. I figured that there was more to it than what we see. I knew there was something at work, calling the shots. Then I learned about the law of karma. That you live more than one time until you get it right, and if you want to come back one more time and show off, that's okay too. I started thinking and believing that, and the more I saw, the more I knew it made sense. It was like going to school: Pass your lessons in the first grade and you advance to the second grade. If you don't, you repeat the first grade again to learn what you missed the first time."[2]

The concept of karma has crept into novels and other forms of popular thought. The television show *My Name is Earl* had karma as its running theme.

Nelson's question about suffering is a serious and vital one, but beyond the scope of the present book.

Any answer, however, must not contradict what Scripture teaches about other issues—in this case, what it declares about the nature of death. Also, science has given us some clues about the possibility—or rather, impossibility—of reincarnation.

Some forms of spiritualism toy with reincarnation, teaching that after death the spirit or soul can advance through various levels of extraterrestrial existence until it reaches the highest possible plane. Other concepts of reincarnation have a person's soul being reborn in the body of a descendant of the individual. Books and other popular media have sought to retrace alleged past lives.

The noted American inventor Thomas Edison conceived of one of the more unusual forms of reincarnation. He believed that submicroscopic "life units" inhabited and controlled every cell of the body. When the organism died, the entities left the body, floated around a while, then reassembled in another organism and animated it.[3] The concept reminds one of the plot device of the Force used in the *Star Wars* movies.

Recycled Souls

Scientology, a group that has especially attracted a following among entertainment celebrities, has its own version of souls reappearing again and again. Originally founded by L. Ron Hubbard, a science fiction writer popular during the 1950s, the belief teaches that when a person dies the individual's soul will be "born again into the flesh of another body."

Humans are really immortal beings that Scientologists term "thetans" residing in "meat bodies" that they discard at death. Unfortunately, when the body dies, the thetan that had inhabited it now forgets what happened during that life except for some vague traumatic mental images and feelings. The residual images will make the thetan behave fearfully and irrationally in its next life unless the person purges them through counseling sessions called "auditing." Unless the individual is "cleared," they cannot advance spiritually up the "Bridge to Total Freedom." If the thetan/soul continues to progress through a series of births and deaths that take it up through higher and higher stages it will eventually reach a point in which it becomes a pure soul that no longer has a need for a physical body.

Scientologists claim that they do not believe in reincarnation in the sense of Hinduism and Buddhism. What one does in one life does not affect in any way the nature of the next life. Instead, for Scientology such rebirth is, as Hubbard described it, "simply time after time, getting a new body, eventually losing it and getting a new one."[4]

Scientology's version of reused souls seems to sense at least dimly the difficulty of passing on memories and personality without some kind of bodily structure to record and preserve that information. As a result, Scientology allows only the transmission of vague images and feelings from one individual to another, but even that ultimately becomes impossible. A soul such as Scientology imagines is really meaningless as a person since it has no enduring consciousness.

Nothing at All

Reincarnation has a long history both in Eastern and Western cultures. But if memory and personality reside in the neural structure as science has overwhelmingly demonstrated, how can they survive by themselves after the destruction of the brain? Any personality that could exist after the death of its brain and then incorporate itself into another person at conception—sometimes repeating the process again and again—would be so amorphous as to be really nothing at all. Or if immaterial souls can retain memories of previous lives, why do human beings then need to store them in their fragile brain cells? And why cannot we access those memories when brain disease or injury seems to erase them?

Reincarnation denies the biblical doctrine that each human being is a unique body/mind unit. The concept of karma rejects the scriptural teaching that each person will face judgment once and for all time (Hebrews 9:27). Instead, like the main character in the movie *Groundhog Day,* people have to keep repeating their lives until they finally get it right.

---

[1] Joe Nick Patoski, *Willie Nelson: An Epic Life* (New York: Little, Brown and Co., 2008), p. 171.

[2] *Ibid.*

[3] Mary Roach, *Stiff: The Curious Lives of Human Cadavers* (New York: W. W. Norton, 2003), p. 183.

[4] Nina Shen Rastogi, "The Afterlife for Scientologists," http://www.slate.com/id/2197279.

Chapter 7

SLEEPERS, AWAKE!

Twenty-year-old Hannah Anne died unexpectedly. As family and friends gathered to celebrate her life in the custom that has developed during the past decade or two, everyone shared memories of her life. Despite their stunned grief, the memorial service became a joyous occasion. The minister leading it declared that the girl must be enjoying listening in heaven to all the good things that people had said about her. Then he remembered something.

"Today would have been her birthday," he declared. "Let's all sing 'Happy Birthday' to her. She will love that."

As a young person I attended the funeral of an elderly relative in a distant state. The small rural town minister described the woman's death as an instantaneous journey from the slums of life's city to a more beautiful neighborhood—heaven.

While such thoughts are comforting, are they biblical?

Many comfort themselves after the loss of a loved one with the thought that they are now happily in heaven, perhaps watching events on earth. But do people go to heaven immediately after death?

The highly-respected Anglican scholar N. T. Wright wrote a small book discussing the recent public fascination with ancient documents teaching an early Christian heresy known as Gnosticism. (The *Da Vinci Code* novel by Dan Brown and its movie adaption popularized interest in one form of Gnostic Christianity a few years ago.) Wright sees some individuals as seeking to use the Gnostic writings as an excuse to offer an alternative Christianity, one that avoids certain objectionable features of contemporary religious expression. While rejecting what he calls "left-wing Christianity," he notes still another danger at the other extreme.

Speaking of some more conservative segments of the Christian community, he observes that while "the American religious right, though it has indeed got its finger on some elements of classic Christianity, is itself heavily compromised down very similar lines to what we might call the American religious left. The type of Christianity which has become popular in the last two centuries on both sides of the Atlantic, in fact, has steadily eroded its grip on the great New Testament and early Christian themes such as resurrection, and has embraced not only an individualism where what most truly matters is 'my' soul, its state and salvation, but also a future hope which is worryingly similar to that of Gnosticism. 'Going to heaven when you die'—or, indeed, escaping death and going to heaven by means of a 'rapture' instead—is the name of the game for millions of such Christians. And when you tell people, as I often do, that the New Testament isn't very interested in 'going to heaven,' but far more with a new bodily life at some future stage later on, and with the anticipation of that future bodily life in holiness and justice in the present, they look at you strangely, as if you were trying to inculcate a new heresy."[1]

Elsewhere Wright has observed that the concept of a bodily resurrection is "a totally strange doctrine to many devout Christians who really do think that the name of the game is to get their soul into a disembodied place called heaven. And when they say, 'I believe in the resurrection of the body,' in the [Apostolic] creed, they think, 'but I don't really mean that; we actually know it's the immortality of the soul.'"[2]

His concern to restore the biblical teaching of resurrection led Wright to author a whole book dealing with the misunderstanding and some of its practical implications.[3] In his book he showed that the Christian's hope is not some sort of survival after death, but of a bodily resurrection in which the redeemed will dwell with God not in heaven but on a transformed earth. They do not instantly fly to heaven after death. Interestingly, the apostle Peter did not consider Israel's great national leader David as being in heaven (Acts 2:34). If not even he had yet gone to heaven a millennium after his death, how could others?

Resurrection and Translation

As we have seen, the Bible does not hold out immortality through the survival of a nonmaterial soul. God created human beings to experience life in a physical body. And it will be as a physical being that the redeemed spend eternity with God. They will become that body either through resurrection or through transformation if they are alive when God returns to take His people home. In either case, God will leave out the ravages of sin from which their previous bodies suffered. We will consider these new bodies when we look at Paul's comments on the resurrection and translation of the saints. But first we need to review what the rest of the Bible teaches.

The doctrine of the resurrection, as N. T. Wright notes, has become almost a forgotten teaching to many Christians and Jews. A 2005 *Newsweek* poll found that only half of Americans thought of it as a physical event. More than a third of those surveyed considered it as something spiritual, an ascension of the soul that leaves the body behind.[4]

The Old Testament has relatively little to say about the doctrine of the resurrection. The Jewish sect known as the Sadducees accepted only the Pentateuch—the five books of Moses—as inspired and authoritative. Because Genesis through Deuteronomy does not implicitly mention the resurrection, they rejected the concept (Matthew 22:23; Acts 23:8). Elsewhere, though, the Hebrew Scriptures do make a few allusions to the idea. Job 14:14 hints at the possibility when the patriarch asks, "If mortals die, will they live again?" Then he suggests that God would call him, "and I would answer you; you would long for the work of your hands" (verse 15). In other words, God would miss His human creation and bring it back to life.

As part of his reply to his friend and tormentor Bildad, Job proclaims, "For I know that my Redeemer lives, and that at the last he will stand upon the earth; and after my skin has been thus destroyed, then in my flesh I shall see God, whom I shall see on my side, and my eyes shall behold, and not another" (Job 19:25-27).

Commentators and scholars have long debated what Job meant, but the patriarch is clearly grasping for something more than just this present existence. The book of Psalms also offers tantalizing hints of something beyond the grave (Psalm 16:11; 17:15; 49:15). Hosea 13:14 alludes to a ransom and redeeming from death and the grave.

But the doctrine becomes stronger in the book of Isaiah. The prophet declares to the nation of Judah: "Your dead shall live, their corpses shall rise. O dwellers in the dust, awake and sing for joy!" (Isaiah 26:19). The prophet Daniel, receiving a vision of God's deliverance of His people, learns that "many of those who sleep in the dust of the earth shall awake, some to everlasting life, and some to shame and everlasting contempt" (Daniel 12:2). The Hebrew word translated here as "many," *rabbim,* means "multitudes," "all."[5] The immense multitudes of the dead who sleep in the grave will rise to meet the fate they have chosen in this life.

Jesus first presents the concept of resurrection in its fullest form. Perhaps God did not stress it in the Old Testament until the world could see its cost—the life of Jesus at the Crucifixion. Or perhaps He did not want to confuse it in His people's minds with an afterlife such as the Egyptians visualized. Whatever the reason, Jesus did point to it before His own death. He spoke of it in two main contexts: that it was possible and He was the source of the resurrection and eternal life (Luke 20:27-38; John 3:16; 5:28, 29; 11:25, 26), and that it was the reward for doing right (Matthew 16:27; 25:31-46; Luke 14:12-14; 16:19-31; John 5:25-29).

Both the righteous and the wicked dead must wait in the tomb for resurrection. Jesus said that "the hour is coming when all who are in the graves will hear his [the Son of Man's] voice and will come out—those who have done good, to the resurrection of life, and those who have done evil, to the resurrection of condemnation" (John 5:28, 29). The resurrection is still future here in this passage, and the grave imprisons both groups. Neither reward nor punishment has yet been given. The righteous have not flown to heaven, nor have the wicked been dragged off into a hell. The righteous wait until Jesus raises them on "the last day" (John 6:39, 40, 44), which would be the Second Coming.

Paul speaks extensively about the topic. He saw it as the key and culmination of the Christian message of Christ's death, burial, and resurrection (1 Corinthians 15:12-19). Christ's resurrection is the basis and hope for our own resurrection. Some had questioned the possibility of a resurrection (verse 12), perhaps reflecting the Greek attitude that denied the possibility of any human being returning from the dead (Acts 17:32). But the apostle argued that since Christ rose from the dead, the same thing should happen for His followers (1 Corinthians 15:20-23). Otherwise, even "those . . . who have died in Christ have perished. If for this life only we have hope in Christ, we are of all people most to be pitied" (verses 18, 19).

Christ's resurrection undergirds all Christian teaching. The disciples considered themselves foremost as witnesses to the fact that Jesus rose from the grave (Acts 1:22), and they proclaimed it (Acts 4:33) even though it antagonized some of the Jewish leadership, particularly the Sadducees (verses 1, 2). To Peter the resurrection of Christ gave birth to "a living hope" (1 Peter 1:3) that was the basis of "an inheritance that is imperishable, undefiled, and unfading, kept in heaven" (verse 4). The resurrection of Christ was so foundational to Christian belief that when a person joined the church their baptism testified to it (Romans 6:4, 5).

Since Christ's resurrection was so sure, Paul could go on in 1 Corinthians 15 to speak of our own resurrection. Christ was the firstfruits of the dead (verse 20), the illustration of our own future. The apostle argues that just as one human being (Adam) had brought death to the whole human race, so another human being (the incarnate Christ) opened up the possibility of resurrection for all humanity (verse 21). Eventually He will destroy the archenemy, death itself (verse 26), reminding one of the ancient imagery of a personified death, such as the Canaanite god Mot.

God's Perfect Database

Some worry that if human beings do not have immortal, self-existing souls, how can God resurrect a person? It is not a new concern. People in New Testament times believed that those who perished at sea were forever lost.[6] Yet John in Revelation 20:13 reports that even it will give up its dead for judgment. In more recent times some worried that cremation would prevent resurrection. But nothing can block God's power to restore life.

As we have repeatedly seen, living things are systems of organization, both in their physical structure and in their minds. They are data or information, and data can be stored or preserved. We all have had experience with the reproduction of a digital photo, a video or audio recording, or the printing of a book. As long as we have a record of that particular form of data or organization, we can reproduce it.

While data chips might get lost or degraded, the record of the organization of who and what we are is kept in the safest place in the whole universe—the memory of God. He lovingly preserves everything that makes us who we are and will reproduce it when He resurrects us at the Second Coming. Those who choose to let God shelter in His unfailing memory all that they are need fear nothing. Death does not terrify them because their soul is immortal but rather because God is. They trust in God, not in some inherent indestructibility of their own. The Creator who first brought human beings existence has the power to make them once again.

Others have expressed concern that if we ceased to be for a time—that there was no inherent immortality to bridge the gap between death in this life and the resurrection—the resurrected being would no longer be us. But the cells and even the physical matter of our bodies are constantly changing, and we are not even aware of it. For those of us who have died, it will be as if we just fell asleep and then reawakened at the command of God's voice. Or to put it into more modern imagery, the DVD of our identity that has set on the shelf of God's perfect memory He now slips into the disc player that is the glorified new existence, and we are once again living and joyous beings.

What Will We Be Like After the Resurrection?

As we have already mentioned, some in the Corinthian church had wondered how God could possibly raise anyone whose body had completely disintegrated (verse 35).[7] In verses 35-50 Paul emphatically rejects such an objection and employs a number of nature analogies to reason out his case. He points to the miracle of harvest. The farmer buries the seed, but it sprouts in a new and more glorious form, looking nothing like the dried husk of the seed. From this the apostle considered the possibility of different kinds of bodies and what he calls glory. The same thing can happen to human beings. Disease, accidents, hard existence, and the ravages of age had their effects on the human body far more in the apostle's time than they do even now. Most went to the grave resembling those shriveled seeds. But as seeds could come forth as new and wonderful plants, so would human beings. Though bodies may be "sown" in the ground in "corruption" and "dishonor," they can burst from the dust of the grave in a perfect or "incorruptible" form. God has far more than enough power to accomplish such a marvelous thing.

Just as He endowed us with bodies suitable for our earthly life, so He intends that we will have physical forms appropriate for our postresurrection experience. "Paul's insistence on bodily life should not be overlooked. Those who thought of the immortality of the soul, but denied the resurrection of the body, usually looked for nothing more than a shadowy, insipid existence in Hades. Fundamental to Paul's thought is the idea that the afterlife will be infinitely more glorious than this. This necessitates a suitable 'body' in which the life is to be lived, for without a 'body' of some kind there seems no way of allowing for individuality and self-expression. But Paul does not view this 'body' crudely. He describes it with the adjective 'spiritual' (verse 44), and he expressly differentiates it from 'flesh and blood' (verse 50). His thought is in marked contrast with that of Judaism in general. The rabbis held that the body to be raised would be identical with the body that died. The writer of the *Apocalypse of Baruch* asks whether there will be any change when men rise, and the answer is 'the earth shall assuredly restore the dead. . . . It shall make no change in their form, but as it has received, so shall it restore them' (Baruch 1:2). Paul will have nothing to do with this view (see verses 42ff., 52, etc.) While there will be identity there will also be difference."[8]

At death we cease to exist for a time. We need no fragment of bone to ensure our resurrection, as some theologians of the Middle Ages argued. The fact that we no longer physically exist is no problem for God. He remembers all that we were. The philosopher Charles Hartshone took what he called a "modest but positive" view of death. He said that all consciousness stopped at death, but that an individual's thoughts, feelings, and experiences are "eternally and vividly remembered by God."[9] But God does more than just remember. He makes those memories a living being again.

Science and everyday experience continually remind us that living beings are patterns of complexity and activity. God can restore that pattern even after it has vanished, just as He created life in the beginning. Perhaps a rough analogy may be helpful. A whirlpool or eddy is a pattern that persists in constantly changing water, and similarly our bodies remain fairly constant even though through our food and breathing we are always replacing our matter with new atoms. Cells die, and our bodies make new ones, incorporating the chemicals from what we eat and the oxygen we breathe. Some biologists suggest that we replace the physical matter of our bodies approximately every seven years. But we continue to exist as identifiable persons.

A whirlpool can vanish when the stream dries up. But it will resume when the water starts flowing again. The rocks and contours of the streambed that causes the whirlpool remain, ready to deflect the water into its endless swirl as soon as rains bring new torrents. But a revived whirlpool is as nothing when compared to a resurrected person.

Even after they have disintegrated into nothingness, our Creator can re-create the neural and biochemical structures that constitute who we are. He reanimates the structures, causing energy to flow through them and make us once again alive. Or to use the biblical imagery, He restores the breath of life to us. When God resurrects a person, He will bring into existence a new body/mind unit that will exhibit a personality in continuity with the human being who died. Endowed with the same memories and personality, anyone raised to life will have no sensation at all that for a time they had ceased to be. But God does even more than just that. He gives us a "spiritual" body. According to Scripture, it is still material. Craig S. Keener reminds us that "an imperishable body, not subject to decay or entropy, would have to be substantially different from our present bodies. Yet Paul insists on the Jewish notion of bodily life (as opposed to the common Greek philosophic goal of disembodiment). God's creation is good (Gen 1:31); it may be transformed, but it will not ultimately be abandoned. This emphasis on embodiment challenges the Neoplatonic spirituality that persisted in Gnosticism, some medieval theology, and some spirituality today."[10]

At the resurrection God restores us free of the damage and effects of sin. He erases things with which we may have struggled all our lives, such as clinical depression and other inherited genetic flaws and predispositions. The Lord removes the biological "clock" in our cells that force them to age and degenerate. They are no longer the victim of the Hayflick limit that tells them to reproduce only so many times and then stop. Our bodies will be "glorious" and able to live in a perfect world and experience things we have never known before.

In 1 Corinthians 15:50 Paul says that "flesh and blood cannot inherit the kingdom of God, nor does the perishable inherit the imperishable." He is not arguing that we will be immaterial beings after the resurrection, but that we will be free of death and decay. Leon Morris observes that "*flesh and blood* is a not uncommon way of referring to the here and now (e.g., Ephesians 6:12; Hebrews 2:14). It directs attention to two of the most important constituents of the physical body, and two which are particularly liable to decay. . . . It is not the present physical body that Paul envisages as taking its place in the kingdom."[11]

After discussing the resurrection of the dead, Paul goes on to deal with those who are still alive at the Second Coming. He declares that their God will transform their bodies. Paralleling what he said about the dead, the apostle announces that the living righteous will have their perishable bodies made imperishable. Mortal bodies—subject to decay and death—will for the first time receive the gift of immortality (verses 51-54). The translated living will still have the same memories as existed in their previous bodies, and they can only conclude that they are still the same persons.

Finally, Paul quotes two fragments of poetry from Hosea 13:14 and Isaiah 25:8.

"Death has been swallowed up in victory.
Where, O Death, is your victory?
Where, O Death, is your sting?" (verses 54, 55).

Paul does not view death as a portal to a better life as did some Greek philosophers of his time. Those who hold that when we die we go straight to heaven would also welcome death if they were consistent in their beliefs. But the pain and loss that all of us feel at someone's death is an unwilling acknowledgment that it is more than just a temporary separation. We instinctively feel its deeper terribleness. The only way of coping with it is through clinging to the promise of resurrection.

Thus the apostle now declares that someday the devouring, insatiable monster of death will itself perish. Eternity will at last begin for those whom God created in His image and meant to live forever.

Paul more briefly discusses the resurrection in 1 Thessalonians 4:13-17. Again he bases everything on the reality of Christ's resurrection. Verse 14, at first glance, might appear to suggest that Christ brings the souls of the dead with Him from heaven. But his point is to assure the Thessalonians that the living will not get to heaven before their beloved dead (verse 15). Rather, the dead will rise first (verse 16), then the living will immediately be caught up with them. Both the living and the resurrected dead will then join Jesus for the first time (verse 17).

The final depiction of resurrection appears in Revelation 20. Neither in 1 Corinthians 15, 1 Thessalonians

4, or anywhere else does Paul mention the resurrection of the wicked dead. First Corinthians 15 speaks of those who place their hope in Christ, and 1 Thessalonians 4:16 focuses on "the dead in Christ." Other New Testament passages have referred to the rising of the wicked, but only Revelation hints at when that might happen.

Revelation 20:4, 5 talks about a "first resurrection" of righteous individuals who "came to life and reigned with Christ a thousand years." Verse 6 declares: "Blessed and holy are those who share in the first resurrection. Over these the second death has no power, but they will be priests of God and of Christ, and they will reign with him a thousand years." Since the passage speaks of a first resurrection, by implication there is also a second one.

Some commentators, particularly focusing on the reference to "the souls of those who had been beheaded for their testimony to Jesus and for the word of God" (verse 4), conclude that God raises only the martyrs here. The rest of the righteous then appear at a later resurrection.

But as we have seen in 1 Thessalonians 4, Paul emphasizes that both the righteous dead and the righteous living meet the Lord in the air at the same time (verse 17). First Corinthians 15:23 mentions Christ being raised as the firstfruits of the dead, "then at his coming those who belong to Christ"—not just "some" of His redeemed. If those in the first resurrection comprise only the martyrs, are the rest of the righteous still subject to the second death spoken of in Revelation 20:4, 5? Luke 14:14 and 20:35 imply only one resurrection of the righteous. Thus if all the righteous dead come up at one time, then any second resurrection would have to involve the wicked. And since Scripture nowhere states they will receive "glorified" bodies—a fundamental part of the resurrection of the righteous—perhaps it would be better to think of the return to life of the wicked dead as more of a resuscitation. We will look at their fate in the final chapter.

[1] N. T. Wright, *Judas and the Gospel of Jesus* (Grand Rapids: Baker Books, 2006), pp. 141, 142.

[2] http://highergroundonline.wordpress.com/2008/07/28/the-wright-view-of-resurrection/.

[3] N. T. Wright, *Surprised by Hope: Rethinking Heaven, the Resurrection, and the Mission of the Church* (New York: HarperOne, 2008). He is not alone in his emphasis. Randy Alcorn's *Heaven* (Tyndale House, 2004), which speaks about resurrection, has sold more than a half million copies in the evangelical market, and Jon Levinson's *Resurrection and the Restoration of Israel: The Ultimate Victory of God* (Yale University Press, 2006) has sought to return the concept to Judaism.

[4] Lisa Miller, "God's Marvelous Makeover," *Newsweek*, Feb. 2, 2009, p. 12.

[5] Joyce G. Baldwin, Daniel: *An Introduction and Commentary* (Leicester, Eng.: InterVarsity Press, 1978), p. 204.

[6] Ben Witherington III, *Relation,* New Cambridge Bible Commentary (Cambridge, Eng.: Cambridge University Press, 2003), p. 251.

[7] Leon Morris, *The First Epistle of Paul to the Corinthians* (Leicester, Eng.: InterVarsity Press, 1958), p. 222.

[8] *Ibid.,* pp. 222, 223.

[9] Gregg Easterbrook, "A Hundred Years of Thinking About God: A Philosopher Soon to Be Rediscovered," *U.S. News and World Report,* Feb. 23, 1998, p. 63.

[10] Craig S. Keener, *1-2 Corinthians, The New Cambridge Bible Commentary* (Cambridge: Cambridge University Press, 2005), p. 135.

[11] Morris, p. 232.

CHAPTER 8

NIGHTMARES

I grew up in a small Midwestern town about 90 miles from Chicago. Occasionally my elementary school would spend a day on a field trip at some site in the big city. We would visit the Brookfield Zoo, the Museum of Science and Industry, and the Field Museum of Natural History. One exhibit at the latter museum especially stuck out in my mind, and years later I told my wife about it. By then, though, the museum had put it into storage to make space for new displays.

But one day I happened to be visiting the Field Museum with my family. To my surprise the museum had reinstalled the exhibit—a large ceramic diorama of the Tibetan vision of hell.

Large pottery figurines of bulging-eyed demons boiled their victims in huge caldrons, poured molten gold down their throats, and otherwise tortured them in an infinite variety of ways, each punishment appropriate to the person's crimes in life.

The tortures on display in the Tibetan reproduction of hell echoed many of the descriptions that some Christians have offered through the centuries of how they see God punishing the wicked. And the fascination with the idea of hell has not vanished.

Some years ago a religious best seller by Mary K. Baxter[1] depicted what the author believed was 40 days that she spent in hell. In her vision she witnessed living corpses with rotting flesh falling off their bones as they struggled to dig in flaming pits. She saw people with burned bones and with worms crawling out of their dead flesh. The inhabitants of hell pleaded with Jesus to save them, but He refused, telling them that they had decided to go to hell by their own choice. Baxter claimed that God had taken her to hell so that she could describe what she had seen to warn others to change their lives lest they also be sent there. (Apparently she had forgotten the message of Luke 16:31).

More recently Bill Wiese had an NDE in which he believed that he spent 23 minutes in hell.[2] The experience had such an impact on him that he has continued to teach and preach on the subject. In his follow-up book, *Hell*,[3] he expands on his reasons for believing in the doctrine and attempts to refute objections to it.[4]

An Uncomfortable Doctrine

Most Western Christians prefer not to think about hell. Clerics and other leaders long used the threat of hellfire to coerce moral behavior. Although a prominent topic during the Middle Ages and into the nineteenth century, it then became a seldom discussed idea. Fewer and fewer clergy preached on it. (Televangelists have used movies about NDEs in which people find themselves in hell as prods for conversion, however.) Hell made people uncomfortable, embarrassed. Others have downplayed the traditional images of fire and brimstone. And a small but growing number of religious scholars—even among evangelicals—began denying that hell exists at all, that Scripture does not teach it. And some of those who do hold the teaching have begun to look at it in new and different ways.

The book *Four Views on Hell,*[5] for example, illustrates the growing discussion on the issue among Christians. The volume approached the topic from several perspectives. In it John Walvoord advocated the traditional literal view of hell as a place of flames and unceasing suffering.

William Crockett suggested that hell is not a place of actual fire, but a condition of total alienation and isolation from God. The wicked suffer because they realize that they have completely and forever cut themselves off from His love. Such a view attempts to soften the horror of God endlessly punishing the wicked, while at the same time seeking to retain the doctrine of hell itself.

Clark H. Pinnock, on the other hand, argued that God eventually destroys the lost rather than making them suffer time without end.

And finally, Zachary J. Hayes explains to an evangelical audience the historical reasoning behind the doctrine of purgatory, an intermediate state in which the dead receive punishment for minor sins as a means of preparing them for heaven.

Each author in the book then responded to the views of the others. As a result of such discussions more and more Christians are reevaluating what Scripture has to say on death and the afterlife.

The Lure of the Doctrine of Hell

Why has the doctrine of hell had such a firm hold on Christianity (as well as other religions) for so long?

Horrible as it may be, it appeals to people for a number of reasons.

Perhaps you've caught yourself saying about the perpetrators of some heinous crime, "They should lock them up and throw away the key." Unfortunately, we find ourselves projecting the same desire onto God. After all, He *could* imprison the wicked forever. Or we transfer our rage, frustration, and anger to God. We have Him torturing others for eternity, just as we would like to do to those who have hurt us. Notice how quickly people will consign their enemies to hell. Like the little child who assumes all other children want a cookie because they do, we jump to the conclusion that God desires to punish others as badly as we do.

The doctrine of hell can also build upon a perverse form of human pride. If indeed we have immortal souls, we can only conclude that not even God can destroy us. He can only imprison us in hell. Contrary to what God told Adam and Eve in Genesis 2:17, no matter how evil we might become, we cannot die. Not even hellfire can erase us.

Others struggle with the issue of how God can possibly deal with the great evil they see in the world. What punishment could possibly balance such atrocities as the Holocaust of World War II and mass genocide carried on against the people of Armenia, Cambodia, and Rwanda? Only retribution on the scale of an ever-burning hell. But that raises even greater problems. When is enough enough? Do those committing such acts—as horrible as they are—really deserve unending punishment and suffering?

Some argue that whatever God wants to do is right simply because He is God. Who would dare question anything that He chooses to do, including unending punishment? At first glance those who take such a position might seem to have a point—if He is that kind of deity. But Scripture paints a quite different picture of what God is like. He is a God of love (1 John 4:8). Would a loving God endlessly torture anything?

What God once said to ancient Israel through the prophet Ezekiel applies to all humanity: "Say to them, As I live, says the Lord God, I have no pleasure in the death of the wicked, but that the wicked turn from their ways and live: turn back, turn back from your evil ways; for why will you die, O house of Israel?" (Ezekiel 33:11). Does His love cease and turn into active hatred and cruelty when rejected?

Scripture repeatedly declares that the wicked will receive their just punishment, that all will face judgment (Romans 14:10) and receive a verdict based on what they have done in life (2 Corinthians 5:10; Revelation 20:12). But is ceaseless punishment and suffering justified even for the most terribly wicked? John Walvoord argues that we do not understand "the infinite nature of sin as contrasted to the infinite righteousness of God. If the slightest sin is infinite in its significance, then it also demands infinite punishment as a divine judgment . . . While on the one hand He [God] bestows infinite grace on those who trust Him, He must, on the other hand, inflict eternal punishment on those who spurn His grace."[6]

Others might suggest that God doesn't do the punishment and torture—He turns it over to Satan. But even in human situations we hold people responsible for what they allow another to do. We would remove wardens and guards who abuse their prisoners. Yet this doctrine of hell teaches that God not only permits such suffering but endorses it. Furthermore, Scripture teaches that God sustains all life—that nothing could live unless God continually upholds it "in Him" (Colossians 1:16, 17). What kind of a being would maintain something alive just to keep on punishing it?

Is a God of infinite love also a Deity of infinite retribution? Is the doctrine of unending hell and suffering truly biblical, as Walvoord and others believe?

The Greek Words Translated "Hell"

As we have seen, the Old Testament has the dead in *sheol*. The New Testament uses several other terms to depict the condition of the dead. The term *hades,* employed 10 times for where the dead are, was also the name of the Greek god of the dead,[7] as well as the place where most of them resided. Greek mythology considered *hades* as a neutral region reserved for the souls of people who deserved neither reward nor punishment at death. The virtuous dwelled happily in the Elysian Fields, and great sinners suffered eternal torment in Tartarus, deep within the earth. While *hades* was drab and dull, it was not necessarily painful. In many ways it reminds one of the way the Old Testament writers metaphorically described *sheol*.

The New Testament says that the city of Capernaum will be brought down to *hades* (Matthew 11:23; Luke 10:15). Jesus told Peter that the gates of *hades* will not prevail against the church (Matthew 16:18). God did not abandon Jesus in *hades* when Christ was in the tomb (Acts 2:27, 31). Jesus has the keys of death and *hades* (Revelation 1:18). *Hades* followed the symbolic rider named Death (Revelation 6:8). Death and *hades* give up their dead to resurrection (Revelation 20:13). And death and *hades* get thrown into the lake of fire (verse 14). Thus we can consider *hades* as almost another way of saying death or the grave.

Donald A. Hagner comments on Matthew 16:18 that "gates of *hades*" is "essentially synonymous with 'gates of death' (as in Job 38:17; Psalms 9:13; 107:18; see too 1QH 6:24-26), *hades/sheol* being understood to be the realm of the dead."[8]

Only the parable of the rich man and Lazarus in any way ties *hades* to the idea of punishment (Luke 16:23). (We will examine this interesting parable a little bit later.)

The term *gehenna,* appearing 12 times in the New Testament, does, however, have connotations of punishment. It is the Grecized form of the Hebrew *Ge Hinnom,* "Valley of Hinnom," a gorge south of Jerusalem. The Old Testament mentions it in such passages as Joshua 15:8; 2 Kings 23:10; 2 Chronicles 33:6; and Jeremiah 7:31. The valley became the site of the pagan ritual of sacrificing children by fire (2 Chronicles 28:3; 33:6). Jeremiah, alluding to the practice, said that God would make "the valley of the son of Hinnom" to be known as "the valley of Slaughter" (Jeremiah 7:32). So many bodies would be buried there that it would soon run out of room and the rest of the carcasses would have to be left for animal scavengers (verses 32, 33). Perhaps because of this prophecy, during the intertestamental period the valley became identified as presenting the eschatological place of judgment (1 Enoch 26, 27; 54:1-6; 56:1-4; 90:24-27).

Also during this time there developed in Judaism the notion of a fiery judgment. It shows up in the many books that appeared after the writing of the last Old Testament book and into the early Christian period (1 Enoch 10:13; 48:8-10; 100:7-9; 108:4-7; 2 Baruch 85:13). Such a judgment usually took place in a flaming lake or abyss (1 Enoch 18:9-16; 90:24-27; 103:7, 8; 2 Enoch 40:12; 2 Baruch 59:5-12; 1QH 3). The association of *gehenna* with fiery destruction and judgment led people to use the word metaphorically for hell or eternal damnation (2 Esdras 7:26-38; 2 Baruch 85:13). Some scholars have also seen such rabbinical tradition as reflecting the memory of the valley as a place for burning carcasses and rubbish.

All the references to *gehenna* in the New Testament, with the exception of James 3:6, appear in the sayings of Jesus recorded in the Synoptic Gospels (Matthew, Mark, and Luke). Three occur in the Sermon on the Mount (Matthew 5:22, 29, 30). Matthew 10:28 warns believers that they should "fear him who can destroy both soul and body in hell [*gehenna*]." In Matthew 18:9 Jesus speaks of "the hell [*gehenna*] of fire." Jesus asks the Pharisees in Matthew 23:33 whether they can "escape being sentenced to hell [*gehenna*]." Also, He stated that it is better to be maimed than to wind up in *gehenna* (Mark 9:43, 45, 47). Luke 12:5 clearly has something beyond death in mind. One is cast into hell *after* being killed. "Child of hell [*gehenna*]" (Matthew 23:15) describes converts even more intolerant than the Pharisees who had led them to Judaism. The single usage of *gehenna* outside the Gospels (James 3:6) depicts the tongue being symbolically set on fire by *gehenna*.[9]

Interestingly, the apostle Paul never uses the term *gehenna* or the imagery of a fiery place of punishment. He describes the consequences of unbelief or the rejection of the gospel as "death" and "destruction" (Romans 6:21, 23; Philippians 3:19). The writings of John have no mention of *gehenna,* and the book of Revelation portrays only a lake of fire. Revelation does not depict the lake as a place of ongoing punishment but as one of destruction.

The New Testament employs all 12 references to *gehenna* in a metaphorical sense. They focus more on the fact and certainty of judgment than on its nature. It is symbolic language rather than a clinical description of the forms in which God will carry out that judgment. Even some who hold to an eternal hell acknowledge this. William Crockett, offering examples of symbolic nonliteral language in both the intertestamental writings and the New Testament,[10] concludes: "When the writers use fire to describe judgment in hell, they use a convenient image that will demonstrate the burning wrath of God."[11]

Matthew 3:12 compares sinners to chaff burned up with an unquenchable fire. Chaff flares up instantly and then vanishes. If Christ had wanted to stress a continuing fire, He could have chosen a better illustration by referring to something that was not immediately consumed, such as smoldering embers.

In Matthew 25:31-46 Jesus speaks of the judgment of the nations. It is the only place in the New Testament that defines the criteria He will use to categorize the redeemed and the lost. Those who do not show love and concern for others He symbolically places at His left hand, the inferior position in the Middle Eastern mind-set. He will say to the wicked, "You that are accursed, depart from me into the eternal fire prepared for the devil and his angels" (verse 41). Jesus concludes the passage by announcing that "these [the lost] will go away into eternal punishment, but the righteous into eternal life" (verse 46).

Earlier, in His parable of the wheat and the tares, or weeds, Jesus states that the harvesters will gather and burn the weeds at the harvest, or as some translations render it, "at the end of this age" (Matthew 13:24-30). The weeds are not being continually thrown into the fire, but are held until the conclusion of the harvest.

Clark Pinnock observes that "Jesus does not define the nature either of eternal life or of eternal death. He says there will be two destinies and leaves it there. This perspective gives us the freedom to interpret the saying about hell either as everlasting conscious torment (eternal punish*ing*) or as irreversible destruction (eternal punish*ment*). The text allows for both interpretations because it teaches only the finality of the judgment, not its precise nature. Matthew 25:46 is not a proof text for everlasting conscious punishing."[12]

Is Eternal Always Forever?

Fire imagery appears constantly in the biblical portrayals of judgment and the last days. The fire that God uses to purge the earth (2 Peter 3:10-12) He ignites at the close of the millennium to destroy totally the finally impenitent (Matthew 10:28; Revelation 20:9). The devil gets thrown into a lake of fire (Revelation 20:10) in which he faces torment "day and night forever and ever." Verses 11-15 describe the judgment of the wicked dead. Those whose names do not appear in the "book of life" also wind up in the lake of fire (verse 15) along with death and *hades* (verse 14), the symbolic destruction of the principle, or concept, of death and the grave. Verses 14, 15 do not say that the lost receive their punishment in *gehenna,* but simply mention a lake of fire.

Scripture clearly portrays fire as God's instrument of punishment, but is it fire of eternal duration, something that will rage and torment forever? The key to understanding this lies in the Greek word *ai nios,* translated "eternal."

Most people assume that each word in a language has only one specific meaning. A hermeneutical, or interpretative, principle that many Bible students follow is to find a clear usage of a biblical word and apply the definition revealed there to a more obscure passage. But while generally helpful, the approach is not foolproof. As all of us know, many—if not most—words have more than one shade of meaning. Sometimes those meanings can be quite different from each other.

Greek lexicons unquestioningly reveal that *ai nios* involves time. But is that the only meaning the word has? Let us look at how the New Testament employs the word when it qualifies nouns of action or process. The New Testament has six examples. Interestingly, all six touch upon the issue of final judgment. Three of the examples cluster in the book of Hebrews. We will examine them first.

Because Christ learned obedience through His suffering, according to Hebrews 5:8, 9, He was made per-

fect and "became the source of eternal salvation."
Christ is not forever still in the process of saving His
people in the sense that He has to do more and more
to redeem them. Rather, what He did at the cross once
and for all time brought them "everlasting" salvation.
He completed the act of redemption at a specific point
in time, but its consequences—what it means for us—
will last throughout eternity.

Hebrews 6:2 mentions "eternal judgment" as one
of the basic Christian teachings. But is it eternal in duration or of outcome and result? Few would argue that
God spends eternity in the act or process of judging
the human race. We would consider it grossly unfair for
a trial never to have a resolution. And punishment cannot be enacted until the judgment is completed, so hell
could not come into existence until then.

According to Hebrews 9:12, Christ "entered once
for all into the Holy Place" to obtain for us "eternal
redemption." Will He continue to offer "his own
blood" throughout eternity, even after He returns at
the Second Coming to take the redeemed home with
Him? Will there even be any need to do so? Or is His
redemption eternal and everlasting in what He has
done for the redeemed? That is, it has accomplished
something that will not be reversed or cease to be.

Christ in Mark 3:29 speaks of those who blaspheme
against the Holy Spirit as having committed "an eternal
sin." Some might argue that such sinners continue to do
it as they spend the ceaseless ages of eternity in hell, but
Christ has in mind here a definite act conducted at a specific and limited time. It is something that has already
happened, since He is responding to those who had de-

clared that He had "an unclean spirit" (verse 30). Although His accusers may still repeat it, it was a sin committed at a definite time and place. The results—what it has done to the person who did it—will, however, last for eternity. Its consequences will never cease.

We have seen a definite pattern in the first four "eternal" passages that we have examined. "Eternal" (*ai nios*) does not always have to mean something of unending time. Rather, in the passages we have considered, the term makes better sense when understood as involving everlasting consequences.

Second Thessalonians 1:9 tells of those who "will suffer the punishment of eternal destruction" because they did not "obey the gospel" (verse 8). This destruction happens "on that day" He comes (verse 10). It will not then continue to keep on happening, but the results of that one day will have no end.

Finally, as we noticed previously, Jesus announces at the end of His parable of the judgment in Matthew 25 that the wicked "will go away into eternal punishment" (verse 46). If nothing else, our examination of the other five uses of *ai nios* to modify words of action or process shows that the punishment here does not have to be of infinite duration, but can instead be of infinite consequences. The punishment, while conducted during a limited timespan, will have eternal results. Its significance will never cease.

Jude demonstrates the same kind of reasoning. It declares that because of their immorality and unnatural lust the ancient cities of Sodom and Gomorrah underwent "a punishment of eternal [*ai nios*] fire" (verse 7). The fire has long ago burned out, but the cities are gone forever.

As we mentioned earlier, some try to define hell and its punishment as eternal separation from God instead of physical suffering from fire. But what does separation from God mean? Is it even possible? The Old Testament has God present with those in *sheol*. Admittedly, this is metaphorical, but it reminds us that it really is impossible to escape Him. Would a truly loving God keep someone alive when He knows that His love would bring only infinite pain and suffering? To do that would not be love, but sadism.

The Parable of the Rich Man and Lazarus

What about Jesus' parable of the rich man and Lazarus in Luke 16? At first glance it appears to offer biblical support not only for a conscious afterlife but also for an actual hell in which the wicked suffer for the evil deeds they committed in the present life.

Jesus introduces an unnamed rich man. The emphasis is on his economic status, not who he might be. The man dresses in a purple outer garment and a fine linen undergarment. Together they symbolize extreme luxury.[13] The wealthy man feasts every day during a time when most people could obtain barely enough food to survive (verse 19). One had to be extremely rich in the ancient world to afford to eat so ostentatiously. The Greek word employed for the feasting indicates a gourmet consuming expensive and unusual dishes.[14] At the gate of his estate[15] lies a beggar named Lazarus (verse 20).[16]

Lazarus, covered with sores that the semiwild scavenger dogs of Palestine painfully lick, hopes for a few crumbs from the rich man's table to enable him to cling to life. But he dies, and angels carry him to Abraham (verse 22).[17] Since the text mentions that the rich man was buried, but not Lazarus, the parable implies that the beggar suffered the ancient dishonor of not receiving a formal burial. But he does have the special honor of being with the patriarchal founder of his people.[18] On the other hand, the wealthy man winds up in the torment of *hades* (verse 23).

The parable does not say what sin or sins the latter may have committed to merit such punishment. By implication, though, it was because he lived only for himself.[19] William Barclay suggests that it "was that he never noticed Lazarus, that he accepted him as part of the landscape and simply thought it perfectly natural and inevitable that Lazarus should be in pain and hunger while he wallowed in luxury."[20]

Jesus' parable has Lazarus and the rich man reversing status. "Jewish people expected an inversion of status, where the oppressed righteous . . . would be exalted above the oppressing wicked, . . . and also believed that charitable persons would be greatly rewarded in the world to come. But this parable specifies only economic inversion, and its starkness would have been as offensive to most first-century hearers of means as it would be to most middle-class Western Christians today if they heard it in its original force."[21] The Pharisees of Jesus' time appear to have considered wealth a sign of blessing from God and poverty an indication of a divine curse. But the wealthy man now suffers while the beggar Lazarus reclines with the founder of the Jewish people in a position of high honor.[22]

The rich man, feeling what he considers the unjust-ness of the situation, now appeals to the fact of his own descent from Abraham ("Father Abraham") as a reason for mercy toward his suffering. He asks the patriarch to "send Lazarus to dip the tip of his finger in water and cool my tongue; for I am in agony in these flames" (verse 24). Abraham, however, declines the request, reminding the rich man that he had enjoyed the sumptuous life, while the beggar had gone without.[23] Now the situation has reversed (verse 25). He explains that Lazarus cannot come to the rich man because a great chasm exists be-tween the two of them. No one can cross it (verse 26). The idea of a vast gulf separating two individuals who can yet see and talk to each other strongly suggests that the parable's hearer or reader should not take the concept literally, but look for meaning on a different level.[24]

Recognizing the hopelessness of his situation and in-stantly changing the subject, the rich man begs Abraham to send Lazarus to his five brothers and warn them so they will behave differently and not wind up in his predicament (verses 27, 28). Abraham replies that if they listen to Scripture ("Moses and the prophets," a common New Testament allusion to the whole Hebrew Scrip-tures), they would escape a similar fate (verse 29). The rich man persists, arguing that his brothers would change their ways if the warning came from a messenger from the dead (verse 30). The patriarch counters that if they reject Scripture, they would ignore even a message from some-one who has come back from death itself (verse 31).[25]

Is the parable a depiction of heaven and hell, of the fates of the righteous and the wicked? Of the nature and reality of life after death?

Above all else, as we approach this parable, we must interpret it in its biblical context. In addition to what Scripture says elsewhere about the limitations of the dead, we must notice that the parable of the rich man and Lazarus accompanies several other parables on riches and how to relate to wealth. John Nolland sees this parable as the climax to Luke's material on the use and abuse of riches (Luke 16:1-31) and the reverse image of the glorious restoration of the prodigal (Luke 15:11-32).[26] Leon Morris regards it as a challenge to "the older son of the previous parable and with him all the respectable who act in the spirit of the unrighteous steward (Luke 16:1-9). They should repent and then help others with their money. The alternative is to use their money in such a way as to secure eternal condemnation."[27]

Fred B. Craddock believes that Luke uses the story to comment on the Pharisees' attitude toward wealth. They accepted without exception the book of Deuteronomy's view that wealth was an indication of God's blessing and poverty a curse (Deuteronomy 28:3, 4). But the rich man of the parable ignores the Pentateuchal command that God's people should share their wealth with the poor (Leviticus 19:9, 10; Deuteronomy 15:7-11).[28]

Craddock also points out that the first part of the parable echoes stories that appear in several cultures, reflecting folk beliefs about the afterlife and the condition of the dead. He warns that "the preacher will want to avoid getting reduced into using descriptions of the fate of the two men as providing revealed truth on the state of the dead. In other words, this is not a text for a sermon on 'Five Minutes After Death.'"[29] Or in the words of still another Bible commentator, "The story is a parable, and therefore does not necessarily give literal information about conditions in the next life."[30]

Jesus may have had still another reason for using the parable. Evidence suggests that stories like it had been circulating for some time in Judaism. Jonathan Lunde, who does hold the traditional concepts of heaven and hell, still acknowledges that "if Jesus did make use of existing tradition, his point may have been the distinctive feature of the parable—the impossibility of a resurrection to convince the 'brothers' to listen to the prophets—rather than to describe eschatological conditions."[31] The brothers would not change their attitude toward the poor even if someone came back from the dead to warn them otherwise.

The safest approach to the story of the rich man and Lazarus is to view it in light of its teaching on wealth and on sinful peoples' hardened resistance to God's teachings, and thus not try to mine it for information on the afterlife. The whole teaching of Scripture must determine how we interpret the parable. N. T. Wright cautions "that to take the scene of Abraham, the rich man, and Lazarus literally is about as sensible as trying to find out the name of the prodigal son. Jesus simply didn't say very much about the future life; He was, after all, primarily concerned to announce that God's kingdom was coming 'on earth as in heaven.' "[32]

The Idea of Hell Enters Christianity

If there is no place for eternal hellfire like that of popular belief, how did the concept ever enter Christianity in the first place? A number of pagan strands of thought began to influence early Christian thinking.

And those ideas were a fundamental aspect of the cultural world in which Christians lived—a part of the very air they breathed and which they began to absorb into Christian teaching and doctrine.

One strand involved how the ancients conceived of what happened after death. Most cultures had some variation of the idea that human beings continued to exist in some way after they died. As we saw earlier, the ancient Mesopotamians imagined the deceased as bodiless shades in a dark, dry, and dusty underworld ruled by a special god or gods. No matter what kind of life they had led on earth, all had the same fate. The dead could help or harm the living, but they could never inhabit a body again. And they were immortal in a limited way.

The Egyptians, on the other hand, thought of the afterlife as a continuation of the pleasant life they had in the present world. (At first they apparently believed that only the king experienced such an existence, but as the centuries passed, more and more classes of Egyptian society aspired to such a paradise.) But not everything even in their afterlife was wonderful. It also had a dangerous, fire-filled underworld where the dead had to undergo judgment. The Egyptians developed elaborate rituals and magical amulets to protect themselves during this judgment and journey through hell, but if the deceased survived its hazards, the Egyptians expected once again to enjoy the physical pleasures they had known in their life along the Nile. The proper use of magical spells during the judgment could be more important than the quality of the individual's life.

The Greek concept of the afterlife had many similarities to that of the Mesopotamians. It also was a bodiless existence. But instead of one common fate after death, the Greeks imagined four of them: "That of the holy, that of those who lived lives of indeterminate character, that of those guilty of sins that can be expiated . . . and that of the incurably wicked."[33] Those who had led holy lives ascended to dwell with the gods in beautiful homes. The two middle categories could undergo a process of purification, prefiguring the doctrine of purgatory. Only the incurably wicked suffered eternal punishment in Tartarus. Elements of the Greek concept of judgment after death would influence Christian thinking on the subject, as did the Greek concept of immortality.

As the Greek philosopher Plato bluntly put it in his *Phaedo,* the "soul is immortal."[34] Greek thought especially emphasized the distinctness between and separation of body and soul. They viewed the soul as imprisoned within the body and its perception of reality as drastically distorted by fleshly matter. The soul, Greeks believed, never willingly associated with the body but rather was at death "freed from the body as from fetters." To fear death showed that one loved the body more than wisdom. As Plato pointed out, Socrates anticipated his death as a release from the captivity of the body. The philosopher accepted the hemlock "very cheerfully and quietly drained it (*Phaedo* 117.C)."[35]

The Greek philosophical concept of an immortal soul would have a powerful impact on early Christian thought and doctrine. Many early Christian apologists had been trained in Greek philosophy and used its ideas and illustrations—especially those of Platonism—to defend and present Christian teachings. Such Greek concepts quickly permeated Christian sermons and writings and became considered as part of the biblical concept it-self. Robert A. Morey, seeking to support the idea of a conscious and eternal punishment of the wicked after death, compiled long lists of quotations from the early Church Fathers and other early Christian writings to show that they believed the concept of an immortal soul.[36] But what he actually shows is the rapid assimilation of Greek concepts into Christian teaching.

Besides direct study of Greek philosophy, another source that encouraged the idea of hell in Christian teaching was that of apocryphal, pseudepigraphal, and early Jewish rabbinical documents, popular religious writings that did not get accepted as fully inspired and thus incorporated into the Bible. Such books also reflected the widespread influence of Greek philosophy.[37] The Jewish historian Josephus described the Essenes, the people usually associated with the Dead Sea scrolls, as looking down upon the body and believing that "the soul is immortal and imperishable. Emanating from the finest ether, these souls become entangled, as it were, in the prison house of the body, to which they are dragged down by a sort of natural spell."[38] Whether Josephus accurately described the Essenes or not (he liked to compare Jewish teachings to Greek philosophical concepts), it does show the hold that Greek ideas had on Jewish intellectual and even religious thought. It also helped set the stage for the development of the doctrine of hell.

Christian writers and teachers took up both Jewish and Greek ideas of punishment after death, combined them with the concept of an immortal soul, and used them to elaborate the biblical references to the judgment and punishment of the wicked. Such concepts were so pervasive in both Greek and many segments of Jewish culture that it was almost impossible not to absorb them unless one clung tightly to the scriptural limitations placed on the dead. Unfortunately, many Christian apologists and theologians ignored what the Hebrew Scriptures taught as they combined popular religion with the intellectual thought of the day. After all, Greek philosophy seemed an ideal tool to explain what were otherwise unfamiliar biblical teachings to a world with little or no biblical background. But the use of such concepts and analogies began to reshape Christian thought itself. It added meanings to biblical imagery that the biblical authors had not intended.

The Bible writers taught that the wicked would receive their just punishment. But many interpreted the imagery of Scripture through nonbiblical lenses. Soon Christians assumed that such pagan concepts were what the Bible had meant all along. Christian teaching on judgment in some ways became more pagan than biblical.

Alan E. Bernstein traces the development of the popular Christian doctrine of hell from its Greek, Roman, and Egyptian sources.[39] For example, he finds the Egyptian concepts of the underworld as providing the imagery of lakes of fire.[40] Ancient novels popularized other concepts, such as worms devouring the dead (in the *Apocalypse of Peter* and the *Apocalypse of Paul*) and the use of pitchforks to torment the dead (in the *Apocalypse of Paul*).

Although Scripture speaks about the punishment of the wicked by fire, it does not depict the eternally operating hell of popular opinion. In Revelation 20:10 God casts the devil and his agents into the lake of fire. The obvious implication is that they are not already there. They are not to begin any role as tormentors of the lost, but rather God sends them there for final destruction.

If there is not a currently burning hell, how does God then destroy the wicked by fire? We will examine this important topic in the final chapter.

---

[1] Mary K. Baxter, *A Divine Revelation of Hell* (New Kensington, Penn.: Whitaker House, 1993).

[2] Bill Wiese, *23 Minutes in Hell* (Lake Mary, Fla.: Charisma House, 2006).

[3] (Lake Mary, Fla.: Charisma House, 2008).

[4] Interestingly, at least one bookstore in a national chain included it along with Don Piper's *90 Minutes in Heaven* as a part of a display of Christmas "Gifts of Inspiration." Only in the American Bible Belt would a book on hell be considered an inspirational Christmas present.

[5] William Crockett, ed., *Four Views on Hell* (Grand Rapids: Zondervan Publishing House, 1992).

[6] Crockett, p. 27.

[7] Hades was the son of Cronus and Rhea and the older brother of Zeus, king of the gods.

[8] Donald A. Hagner, *Matthew 14-28, Word Biblical Commentary* (Dallas: Word Books, 1995), vol. 33b, p. 471.

[9] Scripture uses one more term to speak of the fate of the wicked—in this case the instigators of evil. *Tartarō* means "cast into *Tartarus.*" *Tartarus* was the Greek name of the part of the underworld in which the hopeless wicked receive their punishment. Second Peter 2:4 employs the imagery to describe what God has done with the rebellious angels who followed Satan.

[10] Crockett, pp. 50-53.

[11] *Ibid.,* p. 53.

[12] *Ibid.,* p. 157.

[13] Leon Morris, *Luke, An Introduction and Commentary* [Leicester, Eng.: InterVarsity Press, 1988], p. 276.

[14] William Barclay, *The Gospel of Luke,* rev. ed. (Philadelphia: Westminster Press, 1975), p. 213.

[15] The word used here denotes "a large gate or portico like that of a city or palace. The house was a grand one" (Morris, *Luke,* p. 276).

[16] "The name means 'God helps/has helped,' and is likely symbolic of the divinely orchestrated ultimate outcome of the man's desperate state" (John Nolland, Luke 9:21–18:34, *Word Biblical Commentary* [Dallas: Word Publishers, 1993], vol. 135b, p. 828). Most commentators reject any connection between the character in the parable and the brother of Martha and Mary.

[17] "Jewish lore often speaks of the righteous being carried away by angels" (Craig S. Keener, *Biblical Background Commentary: New Testament Commentary* [Downers Grove, Ill.: InterVarsity Press, 1993], p. 236).

[18] "True Israelites and especially martyrs were expected to share with Abraham in the world to come" (*ibid.*). Abraham was regarded as the archetypal host, appearing here and at the great banquet of Matthew 8:11. See *Anchor Bible Dictionary,* vol. 3, p. 300.

[19] Morris, *Luke,* p. 276.

[20] Barclay, p. 214.

[21] Keener, *Biblical Background Commentary:* New Testament, p. 236.

[22] "The most honored seat at a banquet would be nearest the host, reclining in such a way that one's head lies near his bosom" (*ibid.*).

[23] "He who showed no mercy asks for mercy" (*ibid.*).

[24] Leon Morris offers that the gulf "means that in the afterlife there is no passing from one state to the other (the Greek implies that this is the purpose and not simply the result of the great chasm)" (*Luke,* p. 277).

[25] Could this be an allusion to the reaction of the Pharisees to the real Lazarus' return from the tomb?

[26] Nolland, pp. 831, 832.

[27] Morris, *Luke,* p. 276.

[28] Fred B. Craddock, *Luke, Interpretation: A Bible Commentary for Teaching and Preaching* (Louisville: John Knox Press, 1990), pp. 196, 197.

[29] *Ibid.,* p. 195.

[30] *New Bible Commentary* (Downers Grove, Ill.: InterVarsity Press, 1994), p. 1007.

[31] *Dictionary of Jesus and the Gospels,* Joel B. Green, Scot

McKnight, and I. Howard Marshall, eds. (Downers Grove, Ill.: InterVarsity Press, 1992), p. 311.

[32] Wright, *Surprised by Hope,* p. 177.

[33] Alan E. Bernstein, *The Formation of Hell: Death and Retribution in the Ancient and Early Christian Worlds* (Ithaca, N.Y.: Cornell University Press, 1993), p. 55.

[34] Quoted in *Anchor Bible Dictionary,* vol. 2, p. 110.

[35] *Ibid.*

[36] Morey, *Death and the Afterlife,* pp. 157-167, 273-279.

[37] For representative quotations, see Morey, pp. 119-127.

[38] *Anchor Bible Dictionary,* vol. 6, p. 161.

[39] Bernstein, *The Formation of Hell.*

[40] The pioneer Egyptologist E. A. Wallis Budge earlier had concluded that ancient Egyptian mythology had shaped Coptic Christian beliefs about hell. See *Egyptian Ideas of the Afterlife* (New York: Dover, 1995; reprint of 1908 edition), pp. 111-115.

CHAPTER 9

THE ETERNAL MORNING

Earlier we noted N. T. Wright's observation that the New Testament does not depict the redeemed rushing to heaven at death but eventually living on a new earth after the resurrection.

But what does Jesus mean when he tells the thief dying on the cross beside Him that "today" he would be with Him in Paradise (Luke 23:43)? The condemned criminal had requested, "Jesus, remember me when you come into your kingdom" (verse 42). Since the Greek text of verse 43 does not have any punctuation, it could be translated, "Today you will be with me in Paradise" as many versions do, or something like, "I tell you right now, at this very moment, you can be absolutely assured that you will be in Paradise." Thus translators have to interpret the passage based on factors other than the presence or lack of a comma.

For example, after His crucifixion Jesus tells Mary on Sunday morning that He has not yet ascended to His Father (John 20:17). He had rested in the tomb since Friday, so He could not have been with the thief in heaven that same day. In addition, the biblical evidence is clear that death is a sleep for all until the resurrection.

Also, we must remember how people thought in New Testament times. Unlike modern Western cultures with their orientation toward the future, the biblical world's view focused on the present and the past. We expect things to get better over time, whereas the ancients wanted to continue the best of the past into the present. The present was most important.

John J. Pilch and Bruce J. Malina, in their study of the New Testament mind-set, show that the book of Luke develops its "prophecy-fulfillment" material from this characteristic focus on the present: "Luke most dramatically expresses his present time orientation with the emphatic comment 'Today.'" They cite as examples Luke 2:11; 4:21; 19:9, and conclude with "*Today* you will be with me in Paradise" (Luke 23:43). The two scholars stress that "the basic time orientation is on 'today' and not the distant future."[1]

Thus Jesus in Luke emphasizes that salvation has already come to the dying thief. The repentant man does not have to hope that he *might* receive it some day in the future when Jesus does finally enter His kingdom. Biblical commentator John Nolland takes a similar position when he observes that "it is tempting to find expressed the view that Jesus came 'into His kingdom' on the day of his death. But it is probably better to correlate the use of 'today' here with earlier instances in the Gospel and see, instead, a statement that still in the hour of his own death Jesus brings salvation (in the context of the present mocking of his pretensions about saving others, he extends salvation to yet another person). This criminal has no need to wait for Jesus to come into His kingdom; though not yet come to His kingdom, Jesus is already granting royal clemency."[2]

Luke 23:43 clearly cannot be used as a proof text for the idea that people immediately go to heaven or hell when they die. Instead, all those who die before the Second Coming will rest in the grave until Jesus raises them either at His return or at the judgment of the wicked (Revelation 20:4-6, 11-15).

We have seen that God did not create human beings inherently immortal. God told Adam and Eve that they would die if they ate the forbidden fruit. His warning was nonsense if the couple could not really perish but only entered some other form of existence. Because He alone has inherent immortality, God has to sustain all life, even that of the wicked. The only way any created being can have total separation from God is through total nonexistence. The wicked can escape God only if He causes them to cease to be. He mercifully destroys them instead of forcing them to suffer the agony of being evil in a good universe upheld by a loving God. Not being immortal in their own right, they can and do totally vanish.

The Bible consistently portrays that destruction as being by fire. To the ancients fire was the agency that could thoroughly eradicate anything. Once the flames burned something up, nothing remained and it was gone forever. One wonders what imagery God might use today to present the same concept. Science now teaches us about forces even more awesome than combustion, forces that can tear apart the very building blocks of any substance that we can imagine. The wicked can indeed die the death that God spoke about in the beginning. They vanish in what Scripture calls the second death.

The Second Death

The concept of the second death was recognized long before the writing of the Bible. Even the ancient Egyptians with their ideas of a delightful afterlife believed that those who entered it could still perish, as much as they might want it to be otherwise. Those who failed to pass the judgment before Osiris and the other gods suffered what the Egyptians also termed as the second death.[3] The ancients believed that the personality resided in the heart, and the tribunal of the gods would weigh it on a balance to see if it was worthy to dwell in the afterlife. If the heart did not weigh favorably against the sacred feather of Maat, a monster called Amemait waited by the sacred scales to snatch the deceased. A combination of crocodile, lion, and hippopotamus, the creature would devour the unworthy. It was a complete destruction of body and soul.

Revelation, the only book of the Bible to mention the second death by name, speaks of it four times (Revelation 2:11; 20:6, 14; 21:8).[4] Death and the grave metaphorically, and the wicked created beings literally, will perish in a complete annihilation of the body/personality that Scripture calls a living soul. Although the time period of their destruction will not be eternal, Scripture hints that it may vary in intensity and perhaps even in length for each individual depending on their sins (Matthew 16:27; Romans 2:6; Revelation 2:23; 20:10). That would meet the divine sense of justice and balance that God has implanted in His creation.

The book of Revelation depicts two resurrections. The description of those participating in the first one clearly indicates that they comprise the righteous (Revelation 20:4-6). They come to life and reign with God for 1,000 years and serve as priests of God and Christ. The biblical author specifically declares that the second death has no power over them (verse 6). He also states that "the rest of the dead did not come to life until the thousand years were ended" (verse 5). By implication those in the second resurrection will be subject to the second death.

After the thousand years concludes, Satan makes one final attempt to deceive "the nations" (apparently the resurrected wicked), and they attack "the camp of the saints." "And fire came down from heaven and consumed them" (verse 9). They now experience the second death.

Revelation 20:10 tells us that Satan and his agents are thrown into the lake of fire in which "they will be tormented day and night forever and ever." At first glance this may seem like unending torment, but as always we must interpret the passage in light of the rest of Scripture.[5]

Evil perishes with those who practice it, but Scripture forcefully reminds us that the second death has no power over those whom God has made righteous (verse 6). As for the lost, they now no longer exist. They will not suffer for eternity. The only eternal suffering will be in God's heart as He forever remembers and sorrows for those who had been so determined to cling to their rebellion and rejection of Him. But God will at the same time rejoice in His love and companionship with the redeemed.

A New Earth

After the final destruction of the wicked, God begins a reconstruction—a re-creation of the earth (Revelation 21:1). On it God places a city—the new Jerusalem (verse 2). It is not one that humanity rebuilds from the ruins of those destroyed at the Second Coming but a whole new creation—a gift from God. Just as in the beginning, God presents the human race with a newly created world and a special place to live in it— a new Garden of Eden, though this time a glorious city. And that new earth—not a distant heaven—will be the home of the redeemed forever. "The final state is represented as transpiring not when believers go up to heaven but when God and heaven come down permanently. The future for believers is bound up with the earth and its future, for they are raised out of that earth (cf. Rom. 8)."[6] As N. T. Wright explains, "Earth—the renewed earth—is where the reign will take place, which is why the New Testament regularly speaks not of our going to heaven to be where Jesus is but of His coming to where we are."[7]

Never again will anyone rest in the grave, for "death will be no more; mourning and crying and pain will be no more, for the first things have passed away" (verse 4). (And how could these things be vanquished if the wicked still suffer in hell? Though it briefly flared into existence with the destruction of the wicked, hell too has now burned out and ceased to exist.)

Earlier we saw Willie Nelson wrestling with the endless cycle of human suffering. The Fall had brought sin and death that led to overwhelming pain. Nelson's question of why it continues to afflict humanity will be answered by God's final removal of all pain and death. The righteous will know the true rest of living in the presence of God Himself as they spend eternity in fellowship with their Creator and Savior (verse 3). The eternal sleep is no more. Instead, the eternal dawn of all that is new has at last fully begun and will never end. It will be an unending morning of infinite joy and possibilities. Those who have experienced the pain of the death of loved ones will remember it as a dream that fades upon awakening—an eternal awakening.

[1] John J. Pilch and Bruce J. Malina, eds., *Biblical Social Values and Their Meaning: A Handbook* (Peabody, Mass.: Hendrickson Publishers, 1993), pp. xxv, xxvi.

[2] John Nolland, *Luke* 18:35–24:53, *Word Biblical Commentary* (Dallas: Word Books, 1993), vol. 35c, p. 1152.

[3] Siegfried Morenz, *Egyptian Religion* (Ithaca, N.Y.: Cornell University Press, 1973), p. 207. Egyptian thought could often be inconsistent or even contradictory. Other ancient Egyptian teaching can appear to imply that some of the wicked, although denied entrance into paradise, could become vengeful spirits.

[4] The concept of the second death also appears in several targumim, Jewish commentaries on the Old Testament text. The targumim explain that those who die the second death will not live in the world to come. See J. Massyngberge Ford, *Revelation: Introduction, Translation, and Commentary* (Garden City, N.Y.: Doubleday and Co., 1975), pp. 393, 394.

[5] Loren T. Stuckenbruck, in his commentary on Revelation 20:10, recognizes that in some sense "this destruction is permanent" though he probably holds to a doctrine of some kind of hell (James D. G. Dunn and John W. Rogerson, ed., *Eerdmans Commentary on the Bible* [Grand Rapids: William B. Eerdmans Pub. Co., 2003], p. 1568).

[6] Ben Witherington III, *Revelation* (Cambridge: Cambridge University Press, 2003), p. 254.

[7] Wright, *Surprised by Hope,* p. 190.

GLOBAL EVENTS AND
YOUR FUTURE

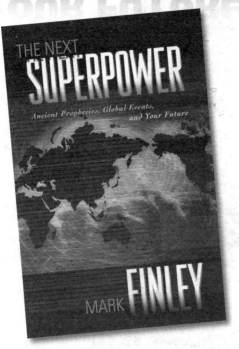

Mark Finley explores ancient prophecies, exposes common misunderstandings about the end-times, and explains related teachings such as the Second Coming, the Sabbath, and the state of the dead—and how it all affects you. 978-0-8280-1918-7. Hardcover.